SATAN'S A LIAR,
I WASN'T BORN THIS WAY

A Story of Discovering the Truth

Cindy McCormick

Scripture quotations marked NLT are taken from Holy Bible, New Living Translation. © 1996, 2004, 2007, by Tyndale House Foundation. Used by permission of Tyndale House Publishers, Inc. Carol Stream, Illinois 60188. All rights reserved.

Scripture quotations marked NKJV are taken from the New King James Version®. © 1982 by Thomas Nelson, Inc. Used by permission. All rights reserved.

Scripture quotations marked NIV are taken from the Holy Bible, New International Version®, NIV®. Copyright © 1973, 1978, 1984, 2011 By Biblica, Inc.™ Used by permission of Zondervan. All rights reserved worldwide.

Scripture quotations marked TLB are taken from The Living Bible copyright © 1971 by Tyndale House Foundation. Used by permission of Tyndale House Publishers Inc., Carol Stream, Illinois 60188. All rights reserved. The Living Bible, TLB, and the The Living Bible logo are registered trademarks of Tyndale House Publishers.

Scripture quotations marked AMP are taken from the Amplified® Bible, Copyright © 2015 by The Lockman Foundation Used by permission." (www.Lockman.org)

ISBN− 13:978-0692561676
ISBN− 10:0692561676

This book is a "Must Read'. It breaches a subject that is very relevant to our current times and culture. Whether you or someone you know is struggling with sin of any kind in this world (which is all of us), this book is for you. With honesty and simplicity, Cindy shares her story and uses God's Word to lay out a plan to win the battle. To say that this book will change your life may be an overstatement, but it will point you directly to Jesus Christ, the only one who can.

Larry Wood (Larry Wood & the Trail of Life Band)

This is one of the most inspiring, heartfelt books I've been blessed to read. God met Cindy right where she was. Cindy invites each of us to join her on her journey. Although this is Cindy's walk, I found as I was reading, a desire for more of God. I believe through her experiences that I too had a purpose and God's timing is always my right time. God has promised to change us, Glory to Glory. Indeed he will change anyone that calls upon Him. This book is filled with hope of God's biblical truths. This is a must read. Every page contains hope and love.

Linda Gore
Hand by Hand Street Ministry

Cindy McCormick's book SATAN'S A LIAR, I WASN'T BORN THIS WAY, shares how she came to Christ and left the lesbian life style. This book can help many people that are fighting any addition or temptation. I highly recommend it.

Norma Bonds
Host of the radio ministry A Woman's Special Touch.

CONTENTS

Part 3: The Battle Plan

ACKNOWLEDGEMENTS

Mom, I'm so proud of the Christian woman you are becoming. Thank you for raising me to be a strong and courageous woman. Thank you also for the many months of encouragement you gave me while writing this book.

Sisters in Christ, Fern and Melody, you two have taught me so much. Thank you for your constant support, prayers, and the many hours you spent going over each draft of the book.

Sister in Christ, Liz, you always have an answer when I need one. Thank you for your help with the photos.

Sister in Christ, Gloria, I thank God He gave you the gift of encouragement. Thank you for taking the time to mentor me.

Pastor, Dennis, and his wife, Suzie, thank you for accepting me into your church with open arms. Your prayers, encouragement and support of this book were really appreciated.

Sister in Christ and editor, Julie, thank you for helping me complete this journey.

I would also like to thank Joyce Meyer for having the courage to be so transparent in your teaching. Your transparency gives all of us the strength to know whatever our background, God can still use us for his glory.

Always remember, "Greater is He who is in me than he who is in the world!" 1 John 4:4

Introduction

One day, in the summer of 2015, I was walking around the side of my house when I heard God's voice in my spirit, saying "The time is now." Immediately, I knew God wanted me to write this book. Prior to this time, I had never entertained any thought of writing a book. In fact, I had been reluctant to share the darkness of my past. My past was behind me and I was happy to leave it there.

However, wanting to be obedient to God, I swallowed my pride and started writing. It took seven months to complete this book and while writing it I felt driven and I discovered a passion inside of me that I was unaware I had.

Satan knows how powerful our testimony can be, so he uses condemning thoughts of shame to keep us silent and powerless.

I refuse to stay silent any longer. As a result of writing this book, I've discovered that through the process of bringing my darkness into the light, I have gained freedom from the shame of it.

I don't believe it's a coincidence you have this book in your hands. You are very important to God, He loves you and wants a personal relationship with you. At this very moment He is reaching out to you.

Satan might be giving you a condemning thought right now, telling you this book can't help you and you need to put it down and not read it. Don't listen to him!

We all have a story and this is mine. Maybe your story is similar, maybe it's not; but somehow we both ended up at the same place. Prior to being saved at age forty-nine, I spent my entire adulthood living as a lesbian. Why the change at forty-nine? Was it even possible to gain freedom from the bondage of homosexuality at that age?

Well here is my story and I hope you'll see that YES, it is possible to break free from the bondage of homosexuality and same-sex attractions. I'm living proof of it.

How did it happen? Well I'm getting a little ahead of myself. Let's go back to the beginning…

PART I:

My Story

Chapter One

The Beginning

The mother of the child was just a child herself, a fifteen-year-old girl screaming with fear and pain with each contraction. The father stood in the hallway, a sixteen-year-old boy watching the coffee flow from the coffee machine onto the floor of the hospital, as he held the empty cup he should have placed under the dispenser in his shaking hand. With the last contraction, a baby girl appeared, my lungs filled with air and my journey began.

One year later, as my parents started to leave my grandparent's house, tears filled my eyes when my leg, hidden under a blanket, was pinched. The tears streaming down my face convinced my grandparents I was crying because I didn't want to leave them. As my grandmother took me from my mother's arms, smiles came across my parents faces, for the next few days they were once again free from the responsibilities of caring for a baby.

When I was almost two and a half years old, there was an addition to our family, my brother was born. At the time my father worked the night shift at the rail road, so he bought a large German Shepard named King, to protect the family while he was away. One day while I was playing with King in the front yard, he started running in circles around me. King was attached to a tree with a long rope and as he ran around me, the rope started wrapping around my neck, becoming increasingly tighter. My mother was on the front porch when she noticed my lifeless body lying on the ground. I wasn't breathing when she loosened the rope from my neck. In a panic she started running, with me in her arms, to the neighbor's house. She jumped over the short hedge between the neighbor's house and ours, my body was jolted as her feet hit the ground and I gasped for air. I survived, however for the remainder of my life I would see a permanent reminder of that day every time I looked in the mirror and saw the scar on the right side of my neck from the rope burn.

Because my parents were so young, during the early years of my childhood, my brother and I spent almost as much time with both of my grandparents as we did with my parents. Finally the stress and strain of having a family became too much for my parents and they divorced. It was decided that I would live with my mother and my brother would live with my father. I was three and a half years old at the time.

By the time I turned five years old, my mother had remarried and we had moved with my stepfather to a new town.

I can't really pinpoint when it happened, but sometime around six or seven years old, I realized I was attracted to girls my age. At the time, homosexuality was pretty much unheard of, but somehow I knew I should keep my feelings to myself. Because of my attraction to girls at such a young age, really as long as I could remember, I was convinced I was born gay.

Growing up I felt different from the other kids. I was extremely conscious of my physical interactions with my female friends. I did not want to do something that would "give my homosexuality away".

My family never attended church nor did we talk about God in our home. My father's parents attended church and when I visited I would go with them. However, their church attendance seemed to be centered more around "obligation" than actually attending because they had a strong Christian faith or desiring to have any type of a personal relationship with God. I never noticed any difference between my grandparents and their secular friends. My grandfather enjoyed his cocktails before dinner and had his bar set-up in the family room. They had a porcelain statue of a young Hawaiian girl on top of the organ in their living room. The Hawaiian girl was only wearing a skirt, her breasts were exposed. Occasionally the Father from the church was invited over for dinner. The Hawaiian girl was never put away during those visits. Even as a child, I always thought it was a little odd.

Rhonda and I were friends in third grade. Rhonda's parents took me with them when they attended church. One night I went with Rhonda to some type of youth class. During the class all of us kids sat in a circle and took turns reading verses from the King James Bible[1]. Since I had never had the Bible read to me as a child, I had never heard the formal names in the Bible before and had no idea how to pronounce them. I stuttered and stammered while trying to pronounce the names. I felt my face flush as all the kids started laughing at me. I felt somewhat relieved, when by fourth grade, Rhonda and her parents moved away and my church attendance ended.

In the 60's and 70's people didn't talk about homosexuality. Because I didn't know anyone else who was gay, I grew up feeling isolated and thought I was "the only one".

Just before I started high school, my mother and step father divorced. My mother left me at my grandparent's house for the summer and took off with her new boyfriend on the horse racing circuit. Up until that time, I had had a close relationship with my mother. All of a sudden my world was turned upside down. It felt like the longest summer of my life.

At the end of the summer, my mother and her new boyfriend returned home, and I went to live with them on her new boyfriend's ranch. Within 6 months the boyfriend molested me. When I finally got the nerve to tell my mother what her boyfriend had done, she confronted him and he denied it. There must have been some type of an agreement made between my parents, because the next thing I knew I was living with my father and my brother was living with my mother and her boyfriend.

My father was married to his third wife at the time. She was young, maybe seven or eight years older than me. I had never been close to my father and had not really spent that much time with him growing up. Luckily his parents lived across the street and I would frequently visit their house. They were like a second set of parents to me and within a couple of months I was living with them full time.

I was always an extremely shy child and when I started my new high school, I fell in with the outcast kids. The kids I was hanging out with started smoking pot and so did I. We spent a lot of time hanging out and getting stoned.

By the end of my sophomore year in high school, my grandparents and I weren't getting along that well, so I returned to living with my mother, her boyfriend and my brother. I rationalized to myself, that since my brother was also living there I would be able to keep away from my mother's boyfriend.

I was still dealing with my sexual attractions to other girls. As I began to mature the feelings became stronger and stronger, causing an intense emotional pain.

Finally, my emotional pain became so intense I began cutting the back of my hands with a knife. I don't even really recall how it started, it just seemed to happen one day. I never knew of anyone who had cut themselves. Although there was external pain associated with the cutting, there was also some type of release of the emotional pain I was feeling.

It was decided that I needed some professional help. As I rode in the car to the psychiatrist office, with my mother and her boyfriend, I looked down at my hands bandaged with white gauze, wondering what was going to happen next. When we arrived at the psychiatrist's office, my mother's boyfriend accompanied me inside. I'm sitting in the office alongside the guy who molested me and my name is called. My mother's boyfriend tells me to wait in the lobby while he speaks to the psychiatrist alone. I'm thinking to myself, "Oh great, who knows what he's going to tell him."

When my mother's boyfriend exited the office, I hesitantly walked in with my heart racing. At some point in my conversation with the psychiatrist, I get the nerve to tell him I think I'm gay. "How do you know you don't want to be with a boy, have you ever had intercourse with a boy?" "No I haven't, I just know I'm attracted to girls." He went on to tell me how great having sexual intercourse with the opposite sex was and stated he was starting to get turned on just thinking about it. "Oh great," I'm thinking to myself, hoping he wasn't going to suggest that he and I have intercourse in his office.

I guess at some point in our conversation, I convinced him I really was attracted to girls and he finally ended the session by telling me it was ok to be attracted to girls and being gay wasn't wrong. Luckily I never had to meet with him again.

Drinking alcohol soon replaced the cutting. Sometimes I would drink so much I would experience blackouts, not recalling what I had done while drinking.

During my senior year in high school, my mother, her boyfriend, my brother and I moved to a small Sierra Nevada town in Northern California. The entire population of the town was less than 300 people. One day while perusing the books in the general store, a purple paperback book caught my eye. I picked it up and my heart started racing when I discovered it was an autobiography about a lesbian couple living in San Francisco. With all the courage I could muster, I took the book to the front counter hoping the owner of the store wouldn't think I was one of "those". After leaving the store with the book, I practically ran home so I could start reading it. All of a sudden the gay world opened up before my eyes. I wasn't the "only one," there were more, a lot more, and they all seemed to be living in San Francisco. I resolved that somehow I needed to get to San Francisco. Little did I know that day would soon come.

By the time I started college in 1976, more people were "coming out of the closet".

In 1977, San Francisco Supervisor, Harvey Milk,[2] was the first openly gay politician elected to office in California. A year later, when Dan White[3] assassinated Supervisor Milk; many gays, including myself, perceived the assassination as an attack on the gay community.

The following year, I marched in my first Gay Pride Parade in San Francisco with the "gay club" from college. I had never seen so many gay people. There were thousands marching in the street and lining the parade route. Due to Harvey Milk's assassination, I was somewhat apprehensive and while marching, I found myself scanning the rooftops as I walked, hoping none of Dan White's friends were looking for someone to take a shot at.

Although I was amazed by the number of people at the parade, I was also shocked by some of the outrageous things I saw. Drag queens, nudity and men bound in black leather. My feelings were mixed between the exhilaration of finally finding my "community" and disgust with what some members of "my community" were involved in. Even though I did not agree with everything I saw during that first Gay Parade, from that point on I lived as a lesbian.

During the following twenty-eight years, I was involved in several different lesbian relationships, the longest one lasting thirteen years.

Chapter Two

Cowgirl Up

As a child, my mother always dreamed of having a horse. Her parents could not afford to buy her one, so she had to wait until she married my father before her dream came true. My very first memory of a horse, was riding double in front of my mother on a horse as we rode on a trail in Mount Shasta.

When I was in the third grade, my mother, step father and I lived on a two acre ranchette in a small town in Northern California. At the time, my mother owned Beauty, a tall bay Thoroughbred mare. Beauty was so tall; to ride her I had to maneuver her next to a fence so I could jump from the top of the fence onto her back.

There were many almond orchards around our ranchette. After school I would ride Beauty in the orchards. More than once while I was riding Beauty, she would decide she was tired and wanted to go home. She would stick her nose out in front of her, so I could not control her, and trot straight for the nearest tree with a low branch. As I caught my breath, after hitting the ground, I would see Beauty running for home. I would get up, brush myself off and start walking home; where I would find Beauty standing at our gate glancing in my direction. I always imagined she was thinking, "What took you so long?"

Within a year, Coco, a thirteen hand Appaloosa Pony of America, came into my life. Coco and I became best friends, spending many summer days together. I joined 4-H and started showing Coco in halter, western pleasure and trail classes. I soon tired of the slow pace of showing. Growing up I was always a tomboy and somewhat of a daredevil, I wanted to feel the wind blowing through my hair as I ran Coco around the barrels and poles. So I started competing in gymkhanas held in a horse park a few miles from my home. I loved riding Coco as he ran through the arena as fast as he could travel with me holding onto the saddle horn for dear life.

My mother and I moved away when she and my step father divorced when I was in eighth grade. I didn't own a horse while in high school or during the first two years of college, but was able to borrow friend's horses to compete in a few High School and College rodeos.

During my last two years in college, I no longer competed in rodeos and believed my rodeo days were over. However in 1981, the year I graduated from college, I was at a gay bar in Sacramento one night when I spotted a flyer for the National Reno Gay Rodeo[4]. I had never heard of gay rodeos, but I couldn't wait to enter. After a quick call to my mother, talking her into lending me her horse for the rodeo weekend, I was on the phone with the producer of the rodeo, Phil Ragsdale[5], and I entered the rodeo.

The rodeo was held at the Washoe County Fairgrounds

located on the outskirts of Reno. I arrived a day before the rodeo was scheduled to start. I had to drive through a group of angry "Christian" protesters at the fairgrounds, all holding signs indicating my lifestyle was a sin and I was going to hell. "How funny I thought to myself, obviously the protesters didn't realize that I had been born gay and there was no way I was going to hell, because God had made me that way."

Reno was only a couple of hours away from San Francisco and the gay community in the city was always looking for a reason to party. The stands at the rodeo that weekend were packed. I heard there were 10,000 people in attendance. The crowd was the largest crowd I had ever competed in front of. It was exhilarating to hear the roar of the crowd as my horse galloped around the arena. I won the barrel racing buckle and after two days of rodeo competition, I was hooked.

In 1982, Joan Rivers[6] was the Grand Marshall at the National Reno Gay Rodeo and it was estimated that the rodeo attendance doubled in size. One night during the rodeo weekend, my lover and I decided to have a buffet dinner at a casino. I was shocked when, as soon as we walked into the room, almost everyone stood up and began clapping for me.

After the 1982 rodeo, I decided that to really be competitive I needed to quit borrowing my mother's show horse and get my own horse. During my first two years of completion on the gay rodeo circuit, I had become friends with another competitor from Salt Lake City. He told me about a horse his cousin had for sale, the horse had been used for calf roping and would also run barrels.

In the fall of 1982, my lover and I loaded up my van and with the horse trailer in tow, headed to Salt Lake City to pick up my new horse. I forget what the horse's real name was, but I ended up calling him Lucky, a perfect name for a rodeo horse.

Lucky was an awesome all around horse, he loved running around the barrels and poles. Every time I rode him into the arena I could feel his heart racing beneath my saddle. Lucky also knew how to track a calf or steer for the roping events. I continued competing at the National Reno Gay Rodeo for several more years, winning the All Around Cowgirl title in 1983 and 1984. Lucky and I were unstoppable.

A picture of me attempting to ride a wild cow is on the cover of the 1984 National Reno Gay Rodeo Program. It was the last time the National Reno Gay Rodeo was held. The next year it was closed down due to financial difficulties. 1984 was also the last time I attempted to ride rough stock. I decided to focus my efforts on the horse, roping and camp events.

After the National Reno Gay Rodeo came to an end, the International Gay Rodeo Association (IGRA)[7] was formed.

I attended an IGRA forming meeting in 1984, and sat next to a man, whom I knew from attending the National Reno Gay Rodeo, who had some new "gay man's disease" called AIDS. I was nervous as I sat next to him at the meeting, making sure I didn't accidently drink out of his water glass or use any of his eating utensils. Not a lot was known about AIDS at the time. Later in my life, I would become all too familiar with the disease, losing several close friends to it.

During the first formal IGRA convention, I served as the Chairperson of the Rules Committee. I was also President of the Bay Area Chapter of the Golden State Gay Rodeo Association[8] and the Rodeo Grounds Director for the first IRGA Finals Rodeo held in Hayward, California in 1987.

Civic leaders were aware of the financial impact the Reno National Gay Rodeo had made on Reno and when the IGRA was formed, several cities were interested in winning a finals rodeo contract. I recall at one IGRA convention held in Denver, the convention delegates were invited to a party in a penthouse located in the top of one of the buildings in downtown Denver. Where we were served caviar and treated like royalty. Can't say I really enjoyed eating those little black fish eggs.

I competed on the gay rodeo circuit from 1981 through 1994. I took a break and then returned in 1998 where I competed until 2000, mainly competing in the state of California. During my fifteen years of competition, I won a total of 19 All Around Cowgirl rodeo titles.

While doing research for this book on the internet, I discovered that in 2014, I was inducted into the International Gay Rodeo Association's Hall of Fame[9].

Chapter Three

Born Again

For as long as I can remember, I felt as though I had a hole or an emptiness in my heart. I tried to fill it with relationships, achievements, possessions and alcohol, but nothing worked. (Little did I know God was the only one capable of filling that hole in my heart.)

I believed there was a God and by the reactions of the Christian demonstrators at different gay events I attended, I was aware God didn't much approve of my lifestyle. From reading the demonstrator's signs, I knew for some reason they thought I was going to hell for my lifestyle. What I really couldn't grasp, is, "If I was born gay and God had made me that way, why would He want to send me to hell?"

In my thirties, I attended a "church" for a few months. The Pastor was gay, as was half of the congregation. I don't recall being taught any biblical principles there. The service felt more like a "pep rally" than an actual church service. I never felt led to purchase or read a Bible while attending.

When I was forty-six years old, I attended a class in Texas for a week. One evening, while surfing the television channels, I discovered a Joyce Meyer[10] program. I don't recall ever seeing a woman Bible teacher on television prior to that time. I had never before enjoyed watching Bible teachers on television, but there was something about the way Joyce taught that caught my attention. I was impressed with her strength, honesty and testimony. I didn't know it at the time, but I believe God was starting to "knock on my door," calling me to him. When I returned home from Texas, I occasionally watched Joyce Meyer on the television.

At forty-eight-years-old, I found myself once again involved in a dysfunctional relationship with a woman, which was coming to an end. Around the same time, a straight friend of mine gave me a copy of the <u>Left Behind</u>[11] book series and I began reading them. It was the first time I had ever heard of the rapture and I was horrified by the description of the events which were to take place during the tribulation.

Because my homosexual relationship was coming to an end, and I was concerned over the end time events in the Left Behind series and Joyce Meyer's teaching; I thought it might be a good time to take a closer look at this thing called Christianity.

I went to a Christian bookstore to purchase a Bible. My memories of attempting to read the King James Bible in third grade came flooding back to me. I told the clerk behind the counter, "I want a Bible I can understand, written in plain English. I didn't want to be reading any thee, ye or thou." I have no idea what she thought of me, but she showed me a copy of the New Living Translation Bible.[12]

At the time I was living with my ex-partner, on a ranch, across the road from a straight couple we had befriended. The wife was a Christian, and unbeknownst to me, she had been requesting prayers of salvation for my ex-partner and I at a Bible study she attended.

I read my new Bible, from Genesis to Revelation.

It had been eight months since my relationship ended with my ex-partner and I felt the urge to attend a "real church." However, I wanted to go to a church where I could wear my jeans, and cowboy boots, and wouldn't feel out of place. In the past I had always seen congregations leaving church with men wearing suits and women wearing dresses. In my entire life, I had only worn a dress on a very few occasions and only when it was absolutely necessary. I knew I would feel like a fish out of water going to a church if I was required to wear a dress. I spoke with my neighbor, who had been praying for my salvation, and she told me about a cowboy church which had just opened in the town where I lived. The church was still so new it was meeting at the local Vet's Hall.

Looking back on it now, I can see how God had everything planned out. He had His hands around my shoulders and was gently guiding me to Him.

One Sunday afternoon, I found the courage to attend the cowboy church. I was apprehensive, but had made up my mind, so I took a deep breath and walked through the doors with my new Bible in hand wearing my jeans and boots. Once inside, I found a seat towards the back of the building. Everyone was casually dressed, I saw a lot of other people wearing jeans and boots and I felt right at home.

The congregation was so small everyone noticed someone new. Several people came up to me and introduced themselves. Then the Pastor's wife walked over to me and introduced herself. I told her my neighbor had referred me to the church. The Pastor's wife said she thought my neighbor was out of town for the weekend and wouldn't be attending church that day. Then the Pastor's wife took a seat right beside me and stayed there the entire service. That one act meant so much to me and made me feel welcomed.

I started attending weekly church services.

Because the real estate market had just crashed, my ex-partner and I were unable to sell the ranch and go our separate ways. We were still living together on the ranch, in separate bedrooms. I wanted to move on with my life. I felt ashamed of my living situation and tried to hide my past and my living situation from everyone at church. Whenever I got up the nerve to tell someone about my living situation and my past homosexual lifestyle, I was always apprehensive because I never knew how they would take it.

There is a story in the Bible about a man named Abram. Abram had lived in a land for seventy-five years and one day God called to him and asked him to leave his native country, his relatives, his family, his friends, life as he knew it, to follow God into a new land. I felt God was giving me the same call. Asking me to leave my life as I had lived it for the past twenty-nine years, leave my friends and all that was familiar to me to trust Him and follow Him into this new land of Christianity. I answered God's call and accepted Jesus Christ as my Lord and Savior.

After I accepted Jesus as my Lord and Savior, the next step in my Christian walk was to be baptized. I was scheduled to meet with the Pastor and his wife, one day for lunch, to discuss my baptism. However, there had been an accident on the day we were to meet, the road had been closed; so the Pastor's wife couldn't attend the meeting. I was relieved to discover I was only meeting with the Pastor, I had planned on telling him about my past lifestyle and reasoned to myself, if I was going to be rejected, it would be a lot easier being rejected by one person instead of two.

Sometime during lunch, I found the courage to tell the Pastor about my past and ask if it was still possible to be baptized. (Looking back, I guess he already knew about my past from my neighbor's prayer request at the Bible study, however at the time I didn't know it.) He asked me how long I had been out of a relationship with a woman and I told him it had been eight months and I was never going back to a homosexual lifestyle. Then he told me yes, I could be baptized.

I'm very fortunate God had led me to a church where the Pastor and his wife had been so kind to me, I never felt judged or condemned by them.

One month later, I was baptized in the river at the Pastor's ranch. I was on my way to my new life.

Chapter Four

Why Haven't I Changed?

After attending church, receiving salvation and being baptized, I knew in my heart I would never return to my former lifestyle. I also didn't have any desire to be in a gay relationship. However, what puzzled me was I still occasionally experienced a same-sex attraction (SSA).

I prayed to God and asked him to deliver me from the SSA, however, I still experienced them. At one point I even questioned my salvation, thinking if I had really been saved I would have been delivered from my SSA. I searched the internet, but I couldn't find any resources for women experiencing a SSA. I just kept thinking I was experiencing the attractions because I was born gay. I really couldn't understand how God had made me that way, after all I had read in the Bible, but I had no other explanation.

I felt ashamed of the SSA and didn't feel comfortable talking to anyone about it. No one at church ever asked me if I was having any struggles leaving my homosexual lifestyle, I guess everyone just assumed I was delivered from SSA when I became a Christian.

Sin is sin, but I have always felt there was a special stigma placed on homosexual sin. I didn't feel the stigma applied to my relationship with God, but to my relationship with some of my brothers and sisters in Christ.

One evening some friends and I attended a mega church in a nearby city, which held weekly recovery services. Recovery issues addressed in this church included sexual sin; however it was focused on men dealing with pornography. Sometime during the service, before the congregation broke into the small groups something was said from the platform, which had gay undertones and everyone laughed. And I thought to myself, "Really? Don't you realize we're out here? We've given our lives to Christ, we've given up the lifestyle, and we struggle, but need help just like everyone else!" I never returned to that church.

I really would have liked to talk to someone who had gone through this same journey, so I could ask if what I was experiencing was normal. Unfortunately, I didn't personally know of any other Christians who had left the gay lifestyle.

I struggled with the SSA, I never acted on it, but just experiencing it was very emotionally upsetting. I wanted the SSA to end sooner than later, but eventually it faded and I was able to be around the women without feeling the attraction. I was frustrated, desperately looking for an answer, when God provided one.

One night I was having dinner with a Christian friend and she mentioned something about generational curses. I was intrigued; I didn't recall reading anything about them when I had first read my Bible. I knew I had never heard a sermon about them nor had I ever heard anyone mention anything about them in the past. I asked her to explain what a generational curse was.

She told me throughout the Old Testament there were verses indicating God places the iniquities of the fathers on the father's children to the third and fourth generation.

Numbers 14:18 (NLT) "The LORD is slow to anger and filled with unfailing love, forgiving every kind of sin and rebellion. But he does not excuse the guilty. He lays the sins of the parents upon their children; the entire family is affected—even children in the third and fourth generations."

Exodus 34:6-7 (NKJV) "And the Lord passed before him and proclaimed, 'The Lord, the Lord, a God merciful and gracious, slow to anger, and abounding in steadfast love and faithfulness, keeping steadfast love for thousands, forgiving iniquity and transgression and sin, but who will by no means clear the guilty, visiting the iniquity of the fathers on the children and the children's children, to the third and the fourth generation.'"

Deuteronomy 5:9 (NKJV) "... For I, the LORD your God, am a jealous God, visiting the iniquity of the fathers upon the children to the third and fourth generations of those who hate Me,"

Pastor Robert Morris[13] describes iniquity as a motivation towards sin which comes from inside of us. In reference to sexual sin it can be referred to as lust.

I knew from studying my Bible God does not lie. He is the same yesterday, today and forever.

Titus 1:2 (NIV) "... which God, who does not lie..."

All of a sudden, it was as though a veil had been lifted from my eyes and I knew the truth. I hadn't been born gay; I was under a generational curse of sexual sin. I knew there was sexual sin as far back as my grandparent's generation on both sides of my family.

A righteous God couldn't have created me gay. I now saw my entire life, Satan had lied to me, telling me I had been born homosexual and consistent with his character, Satan is a liar.

John 8:44 (NIV) "You belong to your father, the devil, and you want to carry out your father's desires. He was a murderer from the beginning, not holding to the truth, for there is no truth in him. When he lies, he speaks his native language, for he is a liar and the father of lies."

Now that I realized I wasn't defeated at birth because I wasn't born gay, I knew there was hope. Although I believed the generational curse was real, I also knew Jesus was bruised for my iniquities and he was sacrificed on the cross for my sins and curses.

Galatians 3:13 (NLT) "But Christ has rescued us from the curse pronounced by the law. When he was hung on the cross, he took upon himself the curse for our wrongdoing. For it is written in the Scriptures, 'Cursed is everyone who is hung on a tree.'"

Isaiah 53:5 (NKJV) "But He was wounded for our transgressions, He was bruised for our iniquities; The chastisement for our peace was upon Him, and by His stripes we are healed."

Up to this point, I have to admit that although I had accepted Jesus Christ as my Lord and Savior, I had not really committed myself to being a powerful Christian. I was basically living my life as a defeated Christian because of my SSA and my belief that I had been born gay.

But when the veil was lifted, I knew I was in a fight for my life and the battle was on. I started really digging into the Bible. I knew there was a verse somewhere that stated something about God not giving us more than we could handle. And also that He always provided a way out from any temptation.

1 Corinthians 10: 13 (NLT) "The temptations in your life are no different from what others experience. And God is faithful. He will not allow the temptation to be more than you can stand. When you are tempted, he will show you a way out so that you can endure".

Satan is our enemy and at the seat of all sin and addictions. In the Bible we're told we are going to have to fight Satan and it is a battle. We are also told God has given us an armor to fight Satan with, which we are to put on daily.

Ephesians 6:10-18 (NLT) " A final word: Be strong in the Lord and in his mighty power. Put on all of God's armor so that you will be able to stand firm against all strategies of the devil. For we are not fighting against flesh-and-blood enemies, but against evil rulers and authorities of the unseen world, against mighty powers in this dark world, and against evil spirits in the heavenly places. Therefore, put on every piece of God's armor so you will be able to resist the enemy in the time of evil. Then after the battle you will still be standing firm. Stand your ground, putting on the belt of truth and the body armor of God's righteousness. For shoes, put on the peace that comes from the Good News so that you will be fully prepared. In addition to all of these, hold up the shield of faith to stop the fiery arrows of the devil. Put on salvation as your helmet, and take the sword of the Spirit, which is the word of God. Pray in the Spirit at all times and on every occasion. Stay alert and be persistent in your prayers for all believers everywhere."

I put on God's full armor, and then some, and went to battle with Satan. I started really studying the Word, renewing my mind, taking control of my thoughts, confessing the Word on a daily basis, worshiping God, listening to contemporary Christian music, fasting, praying prayers to defeat my strongholds, guarding my sight and praying in my holy prayer language. When stating my daily confessions, I didn't say I'm not gay. I confessed God's love for me, how I was a new creature in Christ, the faith I had in God's promises and my commitment to Him. (I go into great detail about the full armor of God I used to defeat Satan in Section 3 "The Battle Plan".)

Although leaving the gay lifestyle is a battle, let me assure you that with each win, the battle becomes easier and easier.

So that brings me to where I presently am. I love God with all my heart and soul. I am confident about where I'll be spending eternity. I attend church, Bible studies and play the guitar on the worship team.

God continues to show me His love and mercies.

Although I have experienced SSA in the past, it hasn't been a constant struggle. I have experienced SSA on four occasions over the past eight years. Will your experience be the same as mine? I don't know, but I do know that SSA is just Satan's attempt at keeping us from God's plan for our lives.

1 Peter 5:8 (NLT) "Stay alert! Watch out for your great enemy, the devil. He prowls around like a roaring lion, looking for someone to devour."

Because I have given my life to Jesus, Satan no longer has authority over my life. Because of my sinful nature, I have a weakness in the area of SSA; however, Jesus has set me free from this sin's power over my life. I no longer have to give into that weakness. God has provided me a way out of that temptation and I'm never going back to my former lifestyle.

Chapter Five

Change Is Possible

I believe that I didn't die at age three, when King wrapped the rope around my neck, because God had a plan for my life. I sometimes think it would have been nice to have had a family and children, but looking back on my life as I sit here typing these pages, I understand I had to go through my life as a lesbian, to be able to reach out to you.

Breaking the bondage of homosexuality is possible, I know because I did it. But what I also know is that I could not have done it on my own. I needed the sweet salvation of my Lord and Savior, Jesus Christ, to break free from my bondage. If you're going to break free, you will also need to know Jesus Christ as your Lord and Savior. It's only through the blood of Jesus that we are able to be victorious over Satan and the sin nature of this world.

1 John 5:1-5 (NLT) "Everyone who believes that Jesus is the Christ has become a child of God. And everyone who loves the Father loves his children, too. We know we love God's children if we love God and obey his commandments. Loving God means keeping his commandments, and his commandments are not burdensome. For every child of God defeats this evil world, and we

achieve this victory through our faith. And who can win this battle against the world? Only those who believe that Jesus is the Son of God."

For more information on making Jesus Christ your Lord and Savior please see Chapter 10 "Salvation".

I'm not going to sugar coat this message and say this journey has been easy for me. But what I can tell you is that I wouldn't want to spend another day without God in my life. He has blessed me in so many different ways and I look forward to spending eternity with him.

If you were walking on a suspension bridge, over a 300 foot ravine, and I knew one of the cables was about to break, I would do everything in my power to warn you of the danger ahead. Even if I didn't know you, I would still do everything I could to warn you.

If you're living a homosexual lifestyle, you're walking across that suspension bridge with the breaking cable. But instead of plunging to your death in the ravine 300 feet below, your lifestyle will determine where you will spend eternity.

Your lifetime on earth is like a small speck of dust compared to eternity.

Every Christian is called to preach the truth of the Word in love.

I once lived your lifestyle, you were "my people". I care about you and where you spend eternity. Over my lifetime I've had homosexual friends die from AIDS, cancer and in accidents. I'm so sad it's too late for me to tell them the truth. But it's not too late for you. In telling my story, my prayer is you'll realize it's possible to leave your homosexual lifestyle and be ready to make that journey to eternal peace and the awesome life God has planned for you.

We can see by reading 1 Corinthians 6:9-10, God does not discriminate. Anyone living an unrighteous life will not inherit the Kingdom of God on the Day of Judgement. Who would be included in the group? Thieves, greedy people, abusive people, people who cheat, homosexuals and anyone having voluntary intercourse outside of the marriage of a man and a woman. Sadly they will all spend eternity in hell for their lifestyle choices.

1 Corinthians 6:9-10 (NLT) "Don't you realize that those who do wrong will not inherit the Kingdom of God? Don't fool yourselves. Those who indulge in sexual sin, or who worship idols, or commit adultery, or are male prostitutes, or practice homosexuality, or are thieves, or greedy people, or drunkards, or are abusive, or cheat people—none of these will inherit the Kingdom of God."

For too long the church has been preaching "politically correct" watered down theology to keep the pews filled and the tithes coming in. To put it bluntly, in the end, this "politically correct" message might make you feel good about yourself and might make you erroneously believe that your sinful lifestyle won't matter to God on Judgement Day, but in actuality it will result in you spending eternity in hell. I don't want that for you.

Any preacher who is preaching that homosexuality is not a sin which will result in you spending eternity in hell, is worshiping his/her own popularity more than he/she is worshiping God and the truth of the Word. Stay away from such a preacher.

Jude 4 (NLT) "I say this because some ungodly people have wormed their way into your churches, saying that God's marvelous grace allows us to live immoral lives. The condemnation of such people was recorded long ago, for they have denied our only Master and Lord, Jesus Christ."

I wrote Part 2, "Discovering the Truth," to share the truth of the Bible with you. I've been truthful in my testimony about my struggles and I'm going to be truthful about God and the Bible. Please do not skip over Part 2. You need a clear understanding of Satan, hell, God and his Word.

In Part 3, "The Battle Plan," I've given you a detailed description of biblical principles I used to gain freedom from the bondage of homosexuality. Although I specifically used the biblical principles in Part 3 to gain freedom from the bondage of homosexuality, most of the principles referenced can be used to gain freedom from any type of sinful bondage.

God loves you and has a plan and purpose for your life. Right now He's standing in front of you, with open arms, calling you to Him. It's up to you to decide if you are going to run to Him or not.

John 8:32 (NLT) "And you will know the truth, and the truth will set you free"

Beauty the horse famous for going under low branches

Cindy and Coco, winning high point in 1970

Cindy riding a steer at a college rodeo

Cindy purchasing Lucky in Utah

Cindy competing in breakaway
calf roping events at IGRA rodeos.

Cindy barrel racing on Lucky at an IGRA rodeo

Cindy team roping IGRA Finals Wichita Kanas 1991

Cindy being baptized in the river

Cindy playing on the worship team at the Vet's Hall

PART 2:

Discovering the Truth

Chapter 6

Satan Exposed

Some people find it easy to believe in God, while others find it easier to believe in Satan. But in reality you can't believe in one without believing in the other. Living in our world today with ISIS capturing their beheadings on camera to broadcast to the world and senseless bombings and shootings taking innocent lives; it's impossible to deny the existence of evil.

You might ask yourself how did evil come into existence on earth?

God tells us in His First and Second Commandments, He wants to be first place in our lives.

Exodus 20:3 (NLT) "You must not have any other god but me. You must not make for yourself an idol of any kind or an image of anything in the heavens or on the earth or in the sea. You must not bow down to them or worship them, for I, the Lord your God, am a jealous God who will not tolerate your affection for any other gods."

When God created angels and humans, He gave them free will. You might wonder to yourself, why would a jealous God give us free will? The best explanation I have is that it's God's great desire to experience genuine love. We all have a desire to feel loved. However, if someone loves us just because they're forced to, and they have no choice in the situation, that's not genuine love at all.

God created an angel named Lucifer (later known as Satan after his fall from heaven) who lived in heaven with God. Lucifer/Satan fell from heaven to earth because he chose to exercise his free will in a prideful decision to dishonor God by desiring to exalt himself above God.

We are given a description of Lucifer/Satan and his fall from heaven to earth in both Ezekiel 28:11-17 and Isaiah 14.

Ezekiel 28:11-17 (AMP) "...Thus says the Lord GOD, 'You had the full measure of perfection *and* the finishing touch [of completeness], full of wisdom and perfect in beauty. You were in Eden, the garden of God; every precious stone was your covering: the ruby, the topaz, and the diamond; the beryl, the onyx, and the jasper; the lapis lazuli, the turquoise, and the emerald; and the gold, the workmanship of your settings and your sockets, was in you. They were prepared on the day that you were created. You were the anointed cherub who covers *and* protects, and I placed you there. You were on the holy mountain of God; you walked in the midst of the stones of fire [sparkling jewels]. You were blameless in your ways. From the day you were created until unrighteousness *and* evil were found in you. Through the abundance of your commerce you were internally filled with lawlessness *and* violence, and you sinned; therefore I have cast you out as a profane *and* unholy thing From the mountain of God.   And I have destroyed you, O covering cherub, From the midst of the stones of fire. Your heart was proud *and* arrogant because of your beauty; You destroyed your wisdom for the sake of your splendor. I cast you to the ground…'"

So from examining Ezekiel 28:11-17 we see Lucifer/Satan is described as once being a model of perfection and completeness, full of wisdom and perfect in beauty. His clothing was adorned by precious stones.   He was anointed as the mighty angelic guardian. He resided on the holy mount of God. Because of his beauty, his heart became proud and arrogant and he was cast down from heaven to earth.

Isaiah also describes Lucifer's/Satan's fall from heaven to earth because of his pride. He desired to exalt himself above God and become God of the universe.

Isaiah 14:12-14 (NKJV) "How you are fallen from heaven, O Lucifer, son of the morning! *How* you are cut down to the ground, You who weakened the nations! For you have said in your heart: 'I will ascend into heaven, I will exalt my throne above the stars of God; I will also sit on the mount of the congregation on the farthest sides of the north; I will ascend above the heights of the clouds, I will be like the Most High.'"

Jesus also confirms Satan's fall from heaven in Luke when he told his disciples that he saw Satan fall from heaven.

Luke 10:18 (NLT) "Yes," he (Jesus) told them, "I saw Satan fall from heaven like lightning!"

Not only did Satan fall from heaven but we're told in Revelation that John, a disciple, had a vision in which he saw one third of the angels swept from heaven to earth with Satan.

Revelation 12:3-9 (NLT) "...Then I witnessed in heaven another significant event. I saw a large red dragon (Satan)...His tail swept away one-third of the stars in the sky, and he threw them to the earth...Then there was war in heaven. Michael (the archangel) and his angels fought against the dragon and his angels. And the dragon lost the battle, and he and his angels were forced out of heaven. This great dragon-the ancient serpent called the devil, or Satan, the one deceiving the whole world-was thrown down to the earth with all his angels."

So there is ample proof in the Bible that Satan was created as the heavenly angel, Lucifer. However, due to his pride, evil came into his heart and he and one-third of the angels were cast down to earth.

As described in Genesis, God created the heavens and the earth. God created man and gave man dominion over earth. God created the Garden of Eden and placed the tree of life and the tree of the knowledge of good and evil in the middle of the Garden of Eden. God placed Adam in the Garden of Eden and warned him that he would die if he ate the fruit from the tree of knowledge of good and evil. Next God created woman, Eve.

Satan appeared in the Garden of Eden in the form of a talking serpent where he deceived Eve into disobeying God and taking a bite of the fruit from the tree of knowledge of good and evil. How did Satan accomplish this task? Satan convinced Eve to question God and His authority over her life. Satan asked Eve, "Did God really say you must not eat the fruit from any of the trees in the garden?"

Genesis 3:1(AMP) "Now the serpent (Satan) was more crafty (subtle, skilled in deceit) than any living creature of the field which the LORD God had made. And the serpent said to the woman, "Can it really be that God has said, 'You shall not eat from any tree of the garden'?"

After Adam and Eve ate the fruit from the forbidden tree, sin was released on earth and dominion over the earth was transferred from Adam to Satan.

John 12:31 (NLT) "… when Satan, the ruler of this world, will be cast out."

Satan's fall from heaven and dominion over earth did not diminish Satan's desire to be God like. Satan's dominion over the earth and his quest to be worshiped as a god is clearly revealed in Luke and Matthew when Satan tempts Jesus for forty days and nights in the desert, immediately after Jesus' baptism.

Luke 4:5-7 (NLT) "Then the devil took him (Jesus) up and revealed to him all the kingdoms of the world in a moment of time. 'I will give you the glory of these kingdoms and authority over them,' the devil said, 'because they are mine to give to anyone I please. I will give it all to you if you will worship me.'"

Matthew 4:8-9 (NLT) "Next the devil took him (Jesus) to the peak of a very high mountain and showed him all the kingdoms of the world and their glory. 'I will give it all to you,' he said, 'if you will kneel down and worship me.'"

So we know Satan fell from heaven because he wanted to be greater than God. And Satan has gained authority over the world due to Adam's disobedience in the Garden of Eden. Because sin was released on the world with Adam's disobedience, we were born with a sin nature, or what you can call a predisposition to sin. You can see this predisposition to sin while observing children. Children don't have to be taught how to lie, take another child's toy or to fight with each other. It comes naturally to them because of their sinful nature or predisposition to sin. However, children do have to be taught to tell the truth, that it's wrong to steal and they need to get along with each other.

Romans 5:12 (AMP) "Therefore, just as sin came into the world through one man (Adam), and death through sin, so death spread to all people [no one being able to stop it or escape its power (our sin nature)], because they all sinned."

Taking a closer look at Satan's character, we see Satan is the unseen evil ruler of earth, he has an army of fallen angels, he roams the earth seeking someone to devour, he is a thief, his purpose is to steal, kill and destroy, he is not only a liar but the father of lies, an accuser, a seducer and a deceiver. He is able to present himself in many different forms, such as a talking serpent in the Garden of Eden and even as an angel of light. Satan wants to be worshiped as a God. Satan is also able to exert his will upon the unsaved to accomplish his purposes.

Ephesians 6:12 (NLT) "For we are not fighting against flesh-and-blood enemies, but against evil rulers and authorities of the unseen world, against mighty powers in this dark world, and against evil spirits in the heavenly places."

1 Peter 5:8 (AMP) "Be sober [well balanced and self-disciplined], be alert *and* cautious at all times. That enemy of yours, the devil, prowls around like a roaring lion [fiercely hungry], seeking someone to devour."

John 10:10 (AMP) "The thief (Satan) comes only in order to steal and kill and destroy..."

John 8:44 (AMP) "You are of *your* father the devil, and it is your will to practice the desires [which are characteristic] of your father. He was a murderer from the beginning, and does not stand in the truth because there is no truth in him. When he lies, he speaks what is natural to him, for he is a liar and the father of lies *and* half-truths."

Revelation 12:10 (AMP) "Then I heard a loud voice in heaven, saying, "Now the salvation, and the power, and the kingdom (dominion, reign) of our God, and the authority of His Christ have come; for the accuser (Satan) of our [believing] brothers and sisters has been thrown down [at last], he who accuses them *and* keeps bringing charges [of sinful behavior] against them before our God day and night."

Revelation 12:9 (AMP) "And the great dragon was thrown down, the age-old serpent who is called the devil and Satan, he who *continually* deceives *and* seduces the entire inhabited world; he was thrown down to the earth, and his angels were thrown down with him."

2 Corinthians 11:14 (AMP) "…since Satan himself masquerades as an angel of light."

Matthew 6:23 (AMP) "But if your eye is bad [spiritually blind], your whole body will be full of darkness [devoid of God's precepts]. So if the [very] light inside you [your inner self, your heart, your conscience] is darkness, how great *and* terrible is that darkness!"

One of the most revealing descriptions of Satan and his destructive power is in the book of Job. Job was a blameless man of integrity. Satan appeared before God and God asked him where he had come from. Satan said he had been "patrolling the earth, watching everything that's going on." After some discussion God gave Satan the authority to test Job, but not to cause Job any harm.

Satan coordinated the theft of all of Job's livestock, and the death of Job's children, farmhands, servants and shepherds. Job maintained his integrity and continued to worship God.

Satan appeared before God again and said Job would curse God if his health was taken away. God gave Satan the authority to take Job's health, but not to take his life. So Satan struck Job with boils from his head to his toes. Then Satan worked through Job's wife causing her to tell Job to curse God and die. Next Job's friends, influenced by the accuser Satan, told Job he must be experiencing his losses and boils due to some sin he was being punished by God for.

From the above description of Satan's activities in Job, we see Satan patrols the earth. He steals, kills and destroys. He is a liar, he uses people to accomplish his purposes and he is the accuser. He did all of this for one objective, to get Job to curse God and turn away from Him.

Because we are in the last days, Satan is increasing his activities on earth.

Revelation 12:12 (NLT) "...terror will come on the earth and the sea, for the devil has come down to you in great anger, knowing that he has little time."

Satan's desire is to exert his authority over you and destroy God's will for your life. Has Satan convinced you to question God's authority over your life? Has Satan convinced you that God does not exist? Or has Satan convinced you that God wouldn't send you to hell for living a homosexual lifestyle, because deep down inside you're a good person? Beware, Satan has been lying to people since his fall to earth!

We only have the power to overcome Satan through salvation by the blood of Jesus Christ. However, if we don't receive salvation, Satan will reign over us. We're either under the covering of Jesus or under the covering of Satan, there is no in-between.

Ephesians 2:2 (NLT) "You used to live in sin, just like the rest of the world, obeying the devil—the commander of the powers in the unseen world. He is the spirit at work in the hearts of those who refuse to obey God."

2 Peter 3:3,5 (NLT) "Most importantly, I want to remind you that in the last days scoffers will come, mocking the truth and following their own desires… They deliberately forget that God made the heavens long ago by the word of his command, and he brought the earth out from the water and surrounded it with water."

Chapter 7

People Are Not Born Homosexual

When you understand God's nature and the sin nature of earth, you'll realize that it is impossible to be born homosexual. So let's take a look at some facts.

God and Satan are real.

Psalm 14:1 (NLT) "Only fools say in their hearts, 'There is no God.' They are corrupt, and their actions are evil; not one of them does good!"

Romans 1:28 (NLT) "Since they thought it foolish to acknowledge God, he abandoned them to their foolish thinking and let them do things that should never be done."

God created everything, including us. God also created us in His own image.

Genesis 1:1 (NLT) "In the beginning God created the heavens and the earth."

Genesis 1:27 (NLT) "So God created human beings in his own image..."

Not only were we created in God's image, but He also

told us to be fruitful and multiply. Humanity wouldn't exist today without procreation. If God had created us homosexual why would he tell us to procreate? How could there have been a plan for humanity to survive? He didn't say "I want some of you to procreate and some not to procreate." No, we were all commanded to procreate.

Genesis 1:28 (NLT) "Then God blessed them (Adam and Eve) and said 'Be fruitful and multiply....'"

God also created us with physical bodies designed for sexual intercourse between a man and a woman.

Because God is holy and morally pure, He can't tolerate sin, He views homosexuality as evil; and because of His righteousness, God is incapable of creating something evil.

Lev 11:44 "For I am the Lord your God. Consecrate yourselves therefore, and be holy, for I am holy..."

So let's put this all together. Since God created us in His own image, He is morally pure and can't tolerate sin, and He created us to procreate, our bodies are designed for sexual intercourse between a man and a woman, the only logical conclusion anyone could reach is that it's impossible that God created anyone homosexual.

So since God didn't create you homosexual, you might be thinking to yourself, why am I attracted to the same sex?

Actually there are two possibilities.

First let's take a look at Generational Curses. Throughout the Old Testament there is scripture indicating that God places the iniquities of the fathers on the father's children to the third and fourth generation.

Exodus 34:6-7 (NKJV) "The Lord passed before him and proclaimed, 'The Lord, the Lord, a God merciful and gracious, slow to anger, and abounding in steadfast love and faithfulness, Keeping steadfast love for thousands, forgiving iniquity and transgression and sin, but who will by no means clear the guilty, visiting the iniquity of the fathers on the children and the children's children, to the third and the fourth generation.'"

Remember iniquity can be defined as lust, a sin that comes from within us.

As I mentioned in my testimony, Satan had convinced me that I was born homosexual, because I had experienced SSA for as long as I could remember. I was wrong. Satan had lied to me and I had bought it hook, line and sinker. I was born under a generational curse caused by sexual sin on both sides of my family going back to three generations.

Does your family have a history of generational sexual sin? If so you could be under a generational curse.

The second possible reason you might believe that you were born homosexual or that being homosexual is in your nature, is because of the sinful nature of earth.

Satan gained authority over earth through the rebellion of Adam and Eve in the Garden of Eden. When Adam and Eve ate the fruit from the forbidden tree, sin was released on earth.

Satan has deceived many people into believing that their homosexual feelings are natural and they have no control over them. They believe that homosexuality is just an alternative lifestyle or that they have been born homosexual. They can't see homosexuality for what it really is - another type of sexual sin Satan tries to use against us to keep us from God and His plans for our lives. And like with any other type of sexual sin Satan tries to tempt us with, we have to put effort into defeating the sin.

We can all understand that we were not created to be murders or thieves or rapists. Why is it so difficult to understand we are not created to be homosexuals?

God created you to be righteous. If you're living a homosexual lifestyle you have made specific choices in your life, influenced by your sinful nature and thoughts you have accepted from Satan, to live a lifestyle you were not created for.

You can decide to leave the bondage of homosexuality. The choice is yours to make. Are you going to live the life Satan has entangled you in or are you going to choose to live your life for God?

Deuteronomy 30:19-20 (NLT) "Today I have given you the choice between life and death, between blessings and curses. Now I call on heaven and earth to witness the choice you make. Oh, that you would choose life, so that you and your descendants might live! You can make this choice by loving the LORD your God, obeying him, and committing yourself firmly to him. This is the key to your life..."

Chapter 8

Why Leave the Homosexual Lifestyle?

In the New International Version of the Life Application Study Bible[14], God is described as "being aware of all that happens, knowing the heart of all people, controlling all things, being a place of safety, condemning the wicked, delighting in our prayers, loving those who obey him, caring for the poor and needy, purifying hearts, rescuing good people from danger and hating evil."

If we want to have peace and enjoy our lives, we need to follow God's plan for our lives. God created everything and He knows how everything is designed to work.

Hebrews 11:3 (NIV) "By faith we understand that the universe was formed at God's command…"

God didn't create us and then say "Good luck, I wish you well, I'll be up in heaven, I hope you make it there." No, He gave us the Bible, the operator's manual for living a peaceful and rewarding life. I once heard the Bible referred to as "Basic Instructions Before Leaving Earth."

Timothy 3:16 (NLT) "All Scripture is inspired by God and is useful to teach us what is true and to make us realize what is wrong in our lives. It corrects us when we are wrong and teaches us to do what is right."

If we take a close look at our lives, we'll realize that all of the conflict, hostility and unrest we experience, results from sinful activity. Lying, lust, greed, jealously, envy, pride and selfishness are just a few of the sins we indulge in. Struggles arise in our life because we are living submitted to our sinful nature and not according to God's instructions in the Bible. We're living under Satan's control and rebelling against God, thus suffering the consequences.

Proverbs 4:13 (NLT) "Take hold of my instructions; don't let them go. Guard them, for they are the key to life."

Remember you were not created homosexual. You've been living a homosexual lifestyle because of the sin nature of earth and lies from Satan you've accepted as reality.

Before we take a look in the Bible at how God views homosexuality, we need to make sure we make a distinction between the people engaged in homosexual activities (the homosexual) and homosexuality, which is the actual sexual act or the sin of homosexuality.

God created you and he loves you!

Romans 8:38 (NLT) "...Nothing can ever separate us from God's love. Neither death nor life, neither angels nor demons..."

So let's take a look at how God views homosexuality.
1 Corinthians 6:9 (NLT) "Don't you realize that those

who do wrong will not inherit the Kingdom of God? Don't fool yourselves. Those who indulge in sexual sin, or who worship idols, or commit adultery, or are male prostitutes, or practice homosexuality, or are abusive, or cheat people-none of these will inherit the Kingdom of God."

Leviticus 18:22 (TLB) "Homosexuality is absolutely forbidden, for it is an enormous sin."

Leviticus 20:13 (TLB) "The penalty for homosexual acts is death to both parties. They have brought it upon themselves."

Jude 7 (NLT) "And don't forget Sodom and Gomorrah and their neighboring towns, which were filled with immorality and every kind of sexual perversion. Those cities were destroyed by fire and serve as a warning of the eternal fire of God's judgment."

2 Peter 2:6 (NLT) "Later, God condemned the cities of Sodom and Gomorrah and turned them into heaps of ashes. He made them an example of what will happen to ungodly people."

Some people are under the false impression that God just wants them to be happy and however they live their lives, as long as it makes them happy, God approves of it. Let me ask you, if you were a thief and stealing made you happy, do you think God would approve of your stealing because it made you happy? What if you were a rapist and raping people made you happy? It's outrageous to think God would approve of you raping people.

Some people think that they should be free to marry whomever they want to. Should siblings be free to marry each other? Or what about parents marrying their own children? Of course not! Why not? Because it's morally wrong.

More than anything, God wants you to obey Him and live a righteous life, which will result in you spending eternity with Him.

It's very clear God views homosexuality as evil and even though God loves you, if you continue to engage in homosexual activities, you will suffer the consequences and be sent to hell. Even if you've lived a "good life", that will not matter.

I've heard people say, "My god wouldn't do that because I'm a good person". If you think "My god wouldn't do that", I can say with confidence that you either don't own a Bible, or have a Bible app on your phone; and if you do, you haven't spent time studying the Bible and learning God's nature.

Let's say someone owes you $100,000 and you go to court and get a judgement against the person who owes you the money. However, even though you have a judgement, the person still won't pay you. The two of you go back to court. While at court for the second time, the person who owes you the money pleads with the judge saying "I should not have to pay this judgement because I'm a good person." Should the judge dismiss the case, just because the person is a good person? Of course not! Being a "good person" is irrelevant to the fact that the judgement had been issued and there is a penalty to pay. A just judge would not dismiss the case based on the person's assertion that he/she is a good person.

God is a just judge.

Don't be deceived into thinking you have your own private "god" who pardons sin, according to your own belief system. The Bible is the absolute truth and there is only one true God, the God who created the universe and parted the Red Sea. This is the just God you will stand before on Judgement Day.

The good news is, because God loves you so much, he made a way for you to be pardoned from your sin when he sent Jesus Christ to die on the cross for your sin. To receive this pardon God asks you to repent from your sinful behavior and receive Jesus Christ as your Lord and Savior.

Heaven and hell are very real places and the decisions we make here on earth will determine where we will spend eternity.

Romans 6:16 (NLT) "Don't you realize that you become the slave of whatever you choose to obey? You can be a slave to sin, which leads to death, or you can choose to obey God, which leads to righteous living."

Chapter 9

We Have Choices

Throughout our lives we make choices. Where we live, what we eat, who we decide to spend time with and what we think about are some of the choices we make on a daily basis.

There are many examples in the Bible of people who were at a crossroad in their life and were asked to make a choice. Sometimes they chose to honor God and sometimes we find them dishonoring God and choosing sin. What's always interesting is when they decided to choose sin over honoring God, there were always substantial consequences to their sinful choices.

Adam was Eve were given the choice to honor God's instruction about not eating the fruit from the tree of the knowledge of good and evil. Adam and Eve chose to disobey God and sin was released on earth.

God instructed Cain and Able to bring an offering to him. Cain chose to dishonor God by giving Him an offering of some of his crops, but not the best of his crops. Cain's sin resulted in jealousy which led him to murder his brother Able.

Genesis 4:6-7 (AMP) "And the LORD said to Cain, 'Why

are you so angry? And why do you look annoyed? If you do well [believing Me and doing what is acceptable and pleasing to Me], will you not be accepted? And if you do not do well [but ignore My instruction], sin crouches at your door; its desire is for you [to overpower you], but you must master it.'"

Noah chose to honor God and follow his instructions when God told him to build an ark. Noah, his family and the animals were saved from the great flood.

Abram chose to follow God when God told him to leave his native country and God showered Abram (later given the name Abraham) with blessings.

The pattern in the Bible is established, when our choices honor God, we will reap the benefits of a good life and when our choices dishonor God our life will be subject to the consequences of sin.

Leaving your homosexual bondage will also require daily choices. Although upon receiving salvation, your spirit is dead to sin's authority over your life, the sinful nature of earth is still active. The daily choice you're going to have to make is: Will you choose to sin? Or will you choose to honor God and act in obedience to His Word? It's going to require commitment and determination. To be successful at leaving your homosexual bondage you will need to submit your life to Jesus Christ, and then lean on his strength.

I recently heard a lesbian on a talk show talking about a friend she had that was a drag queen. This friend had discovered that the lesbian was starting to read the Bible and her drag queen friend had confided in her that he had once been a minister, for numerous years, and had prayed to God to take away his homosexual feelings. When this didn't happen the minister left the church for a homosexual lifestyle.

As I was listening I thought to myself, how ludicrous. Nowhere in the Bible is it indicated that we will not have to face temptations. Actually, it states just the opposite.

Luke 17:1 (NLT) "One day Jesus said to his disciples, 'There will always be temptations to sin...'"

James 1:2 (NLT) "God blesses those who patiently endure testing and temptation. Afterward they will receive the crown of life that God has promised to those who love him."

James 1:14 (NLT) "Temptation comes from our own desires, which entice us and drag us away."

Matthew 6:13 (NLT) "And don't let us yield to temptation, but rescue us from the evil one (Satan)."

Although we will always face temptations here on earth, the good news is, God has promised us that we will not be tempted beyond our endurance for the temptation. He also promises to show us a way out.

1 Corinthians 10:13 (NLT) "The temptations in your life are no different from what others experience. And God is faithful. He will not allow the temptation to be more than

you can stand. When you are tempted, he will show you a way out so that you can endure."

Homosexuality is a sexual sin and just like with any other sexual sin, it's going to take effort to defeat it. It's going to require 'dying to ourselves' and becoming more like Jesus on a daily basis.

So what does 'dying to ourselves' mean?

Imagine you have two glasses in front of you. Each glass is filled to the rim with water. Now imagine the first glass is filled to the rim with water representing your sinful nature. The second glass is filled to the rim with water representing the nature of Jesus. If you take the glass filled with Jesus and try to pour it into the glass filled with your sinful nature, the water representing Jesus will just spill over the top of the glass because there is no space for it in the glass. You first have to remove the sinful nature from the glass to make any room for Jesus.

Our lives are the same way, we need to empty our lives of our sinful nature to make any room for Jesus' nature. That's what 'dying to ourselves' means.

The biblical principles provided in Section 3 "The Battle Plan," will help you replace your sinful nature with the presence of Jesus Christ.

PART 3:

The Battle Plan

Chapter 10

Salvation

The most important and very first weapon in our fight with Satan is our Salvation through Jesus Christ. Without this, all else is impossible!

Throughout the Bible it's indicated that for our sins to be forgiven we must ask for forgiveness and there must be repentance. Repentance is completely turning away from our sin and turning towards God. There is no forgiveness without repentance.

We repent when we decide that we're no longer going to be led by our sexual desires, because we want to follow God. When we reach this decision, we're ready to turn away from our homosexual bondage and receive forgiveness from God.

There are many places in scripture which tell us to repent, the following are just a few:

2 Timothy 2:19 (NLT) "But God's truth stands firm like a foundation stone with this inscription: 'The Lord knows those who are his,' and 'All who belong to the Lord must turn away from evil.'"

Ezekiel 3:19 (NLT) "If you warn them and they refuse to

repent and keep on sinning, they will die in their sins…"

Ezekiel 33:12 (NLT) "Son of man, give your people this message: The righteous behavior of righteous people will not save them if they turn to sin, nor will the wicked behavior of wicked people destroy them if they repent and turn from their sins."

Ezekiel 33:19 (NLT) "But if wicked people turn from their wickedness and do what is just and right, they will live."

Luke 13:3 (NLT) "… And you will perish, too, unless you repent of your sins and turn to God."

2 Peter 3:9 (NLT) "The Lord isn't really being slow about his promise (to return for his people), as some people think. No, he is being patient for your sake. He does not want anyone to be destroyed, but wants everyone to repent."

I don't know why there's a misconception that leaving our homosexual bondage is supposed to be easy once we become Christians. Or that our lifestyle can't really be changed if it requires any effort on our part. Leaving the homosexual lifestyle is not a passive activity. We're literally fighting for our lives. We do battle with Satan through the blood of Jesus Christ.

God wants our love, adoration and obedience. He gave us free will and He wants us to choose to obey Him because we love Him.

I have two dogs, Mitty and Cinch. They enjoy being together, but anytime I'm outside they're right by my side. If I'm sitting on my front porch, they both come up and desire love and affection from me. You see, even though they have each other for companionship, there is a need in both of them for love that only I can fill.

God created us the same way. There is a need in us for love that only God can fill. It's that empty hole in our hearts which was created only for Him. God created that need in us, because He loves us and wants a relationship with us. God walked daily in the Garden of Eden with Adam and Eve. And just as sin separated Adam and Eve from their relationship with God, sin also separates us from our relationship with God.

To cover our sins, so He could have an intimate personal relationship with us for eternity, God sent His son Jesus Christ, to die on the cross for us. We only have access to God through the blood of Jesus Christ.

1 John 4:9-10 (NLT) "God showed how much he loved us by sending his one and only Son into the world so that we might have eternal life through him. This is real love—not that we loved God, but that he loved us and sent his Son as a sacrifice to take away our sins."

John 3:16-17 (NLT) "For God so loved the world so much that he gave his one and only Son, so that everyone (yes that means everyone) who believes in him will not perish but have eternal life. God sent his Son into the world not to judge the world, but to save the world through him."

We need Jesus Christ, there is no way we can be successful leaving our homosexual bondage through our own effort and will.

Satan gained authority over earth through the rebellion of Adam and Eve in the Garden of Eden.

Satan wants authority over your life and will do anything to try and gain that authority. If you've been living a homosexual lifestyle, you've been living under his authority. Satan has created within you a sexual lust to engage in activities God has forbidden. Satan has also lied to you and convinced you that your sexual desire for the same sex is natural; that you can't control your desires or that you won't go to hell for your sins. Maybe he's even tried to convince you that God and hell don't exist.

Ephesians 2:1-3 (NLT) "Once you were dead because of your disobedience and your many sins. You used to live in sin, just like the rest of the world, obeying the devil-the commander of the powers in the unseen world. He is the spirit at work in the hearts of those who refuse to obey God. All of us used to live that way, following the passionate desires and inclinations of our sinful nature. By our very nature we were subject to God's anger, just like everyone else."

2 Corinthians 4:4 (NLT) "Satan, who is the god of this world, has blinded the mind of those who don't believe. They are unable to see the glorious light of the Good News. They don't understand this message about the glory of Christ, who is the exact likeness of God."

But the good news is, upon receiving salvation, greater is He (The Holy Spirit) who lives is in us, than he (Satan) who is in the world!

1 John 4:4 (NLT) "But you belong to God, my dear children. You have already won a victory over those people, because the Spirit who lives in you is greater than the spirit (Satan) who lives in the world."

Colossians 1:12-14 (NLT) "...He (God) has enabled you to share in the inheritance that belongs to his people, who live in the light. For he has rescued us from the kingdom of darkness and transferred us into the Kingdom of his dear Son, who purchased our freedom and forgave our sins."

When we accept Jesus Christ as our Lord and Savior, our past sins are washed away through his blood and God chooses to remember them no more. We no longer have to live under condemnation about our past. Satan would like us to live in condemnation forever. But our sins are removed from God's remembrance as far as the east is from the west.

Psalm 103:12 (NLT) "He has removed our sins as far from us as the east is from the west."

2 Corinthians 5:19 (NLT) "For God was in Christ, who never sinned, reconciling the world to himself, no longer counting people's sins against them..."

On the Day of Judgement, as long as we have accepted Jesus Christ as our Lord and Savior, we will not be judged by anything which happened prior to our salvation.

Man is a spirit, he has a soul (consisting of mind, will, and emotions) and he lives in a body.

Upon receiving salvation our old sinful spirit dies and God gives us the gift of the Holy Spirit. The Holy Spirit gives birth to our spiritual life, in the form of a new righteous spirit. The Holy Spirit also guides us in the truth of the Word and directs us to the life God has planned for us.

Acts 2:38 (NLT) "Peter replied, 'Each of you must repent of your sins and turn to God, and be baptized in the name of Jesus Christ for the forgiveness of your sins. Then you will receive the gift of the Holy Spirit.'"

John 3:6 (NLT) "Humans can reproduce only human life, but the Holy Spirit gives birth to spiritual life."

John 14:17 (NLT) "He is the Holy Spirit, who leads into all truth…"

The Holy Spirit helps us defeat the lust of the flesh.

Galatians 5:16-17 (NLT) "So I say, let the Holy Spirit guide your lives. Then you won't be doing what your sinful nature craves. The sinful nature wants to do evil, which is just the opposite of what the Spirit wants. And the Spirit gives us the desires that are the opposite of what our sinful nature desires…"

The Holy Spirit also convicts us when we are out of God's will for our lives.

There is a difference between conviction and condemnation.

Conviction is from the Holy Spirit, it reminds us that we have done something that has put distance in our relationship with God. Conviction is used by the Holy Spirit to get us back on God's course for our lives.

Condemnation is a tactic used by Satan. It's that little voice in our head that always attacks our self-worth. It tells us we're unlovable, stupid, rejected, abandoned, our sins are not forgiven, or we are powerless to change our lives.

We need to learn to distinguish the difference between conviction and condemnation. We need to listen to conviction from the Holy Spirit and change our lives accordingly. We also need to reject condemnation and realize condemning thoughts do not have anything to do with the person we really are. Condemning thoughts are just thoughts Satan uses against us to keep us distracted or at a distance from God and His plans for our lives.

Galatians 6:7-9 (NLT) "Don't be misled – you cannot mock the justice of God. You will always harvest what you plant. Those who live only to satisfy their own sinful nature will harvest decay and death from that sinful nature. But those who live to please the Spirit will harvest everlasting life from the Spirit. So let's not get tired of doing what is good. At just the right time we will reap a harvest of blessing if we don't give up."

If you would like to ask Jesus Christ to become your Lord and Savior, state the following prayer aloud:

"Lord Jesus, I'm a sinner. Forgive me for my sins. I repent of my sins. I believe that you died on the cross for me and paid the price for my sins. I believe that you arose on the third day and you are seated at the right hand of the Father. I'm asking you to come into my heart. I make you Lord of my life. I want to change my lifestyle. I ask that you take my mind and help me to transform it to become like yours. I ask this in Jesus precious name. Amen."

I believe if you sincerely said the above prayer, you have received salvation, along with the indwelling of the Holy Spirit, who will now live within your heart and will help you through this journey and with the rest of your life. Welcome to the family of God!

The Bible states very clearly that after we accept Jesus Christ as our Lord and Savior we should be baptized as soon as possible. Throughout the New Testament Baptism is always described as being accomplished through the complete immersion under water.

Jesus Christ was crucified for our sins, He was buried, and He arose on the third day to be seated at the right hand of God. Water baptism joins us with Jesus through his death, burial and resurrection. Our complete immersion signifies our death and burial of our past sins and our sin nature, when we emerge from the water it signifies our resurrection with or joining with Jesus Christ into our new nature and life. We are no longer under the authority of sin.

Romans 6:3-7,11 (NLT) "Or have you forgotten that when we were joined with Christ Jesus in baptism, we joined him in his death? For we died and were buried with Christ by baptism. And just as Christ was raised from the dead by the glorious power of the Father, now we also may live new lives. Since we have been united with him in his death, we will also be raised to life as he was. We know that our old sinful selves were crucified with Christ so that sin might lose its power in our lives. We are no longer slaves to sin. For when we died with Christ we were set free from the power of sin….. So you also should consider yourselves to be dead to the power of sin and alive to God through Christ Jesus."

2 Corinthians 5:17 (NLT) "This means that anyone who belongs to Christ has become a new person. The old life is gone; a new life has begun!"

John 8:36 (NLT) "So if the Son sets you free, you are truly free."

Once we accept Jesus Christ as our Lord and Savior and we are baptized, our spirit is reborn and we become his, Satan no longer has authority over our spirit.

1 John 5:18-19 (NLT) "We know that God's children do not make a practice of sinning, for God's Son holds them securely, and the evil one cannot touch them. We know

that we are children of God and that the world around us is under the control of the evil one."

Romans 6:18 (NLT) "Now you are free from your slavery to sin, and you have become slaves to righteous living."

Colossians 1:13-14 (AMP) "For He (God) has rescued us *and* has drawn us to Himself from the dominion of darkness, and has transferred us to the kingdom of His beloved Son, in whom we have redemption [because of His sacrifice, resulting in] the forgiveness of our sins [and the cancellation of sins' penalty]."

Remember man is a spirit, he has a soul (consisting of mind, will and emotions) and he lives in a body. Paul tells us in Romans that after receiving salvation and baptism, we are still responsible for offering our bodies as living sacrifices and renewing our mind. If our bodies and mind were also reborn upon receiving salvation, we wouldn't have this responsibility.

Romans 12:1-2 (NIV) "Therefore, I urge you, brothers, in view of God's mercy (salvation), to offer your bodies as living sacrifices, holy and pleasing to God-this is your spiritual act of worship. Do not conform any longer to the pattern of this world, but be transformed by the renewing of your mind."

Chapter 11

Controlling Our Thoughts

Controlling our thoughts is the second most important biblical principle we can use, in our war with Satan, to break the bondage of homosexuality.

Sexual sin is like a raging wildfire. It starts with a small spark then grows into an uncontrollable raging fire, leaving death and destruction in its wake and never consuming enough fuel to be completely satisfied. Because sexual sin is never satisfied, it always leads to bondage and strongholds.

If you've lived a homosexual lifestyle, you've built strongholds in your mind. The longer you've spent living your life as a homosexual the stronger the strongholds. A stronghold is a thought, outside of the will of God for your life, that you have accepted as a truth and made it your reality.

Satan is a liar and a deceiver. The major area Satan attacks us is in our thoughts. Satan, through his lies, has established within us personal beliefs about ourselves (for example: 'I was born gay' or 'I can't leave my homosexual lifestyle'), to resist the truth of the Bible. Satan uses these thoughts to try and block us from God's plan for our lives and to keep us under his authority.

Ephesians 2:3 (NIV) "All of us lived among them (people living under the authority of Satan) at one time, gratifying the cravings of our sinful nature and following its desires and thoughts."

But once we accept Jesus Christ as our Lord and Savior and are baptized, we are no longer under Satan's authority. Jesus now has authority over our lives and we need to take our thoughts and put them under the obedience of His authority.

John 10:10 (NLT) "The thief's (Satan's) purpose is to steal and kill and destroy. My (Jesus Christ) purpose is to give them a rich and satisfying life."

2 Corinthians 3:17 (AMP) "Now the Lord is the Spirit, and where the Spirit of the Lord is, there is liberty (emancipation from bondage, freedom)."

Paul tells us in 2 Corinthians that we wage spiritual warfare against Satan and we need to bring all of our thoughts into captivity to the obedience of Christ.

2 Corinthians 10:3-5 (NLT) "We are human, but we don't wage war as humans do. We use God's mighty weapons, not worldly weapons, to knock down the strongholds of human reasoning and to destroy false arguments. We destroy every proud obstacle that keeps people from knowing God. We capture their rebellious thoughts and teach them to obey Christ."

You might wonder why is it so important to take our thoughts captive?

In reference to sexual sin, our sin actually occurs first with our lustful thoughts, long before we engage in any physical activity of sin. Jesus clearly demonstrates this in Matthew, where he teaches us that if a man even looks at a woman with lust, he has already committed adultery with that woman. The sin is first committed with the lustful thoughts.

Matthew 5:28 (NLT) "But I say, anyone who even looks at a woman with lust has already committed adultery with her in his heart."

In order to be successful at leaving the homosexual lifestyle, you need to stop engaging in lustful thoughts.

You might think that watching pornography, masturbating or simply thinking lustful thoughts about someone you are attracted to are all harmless activities. Satan has lied to you about this! When you choose to think lustful thoughts you have already committed a sin, you are opening the door to Satan and he will gladly come in.

So what does taking every thought captive mean?

We need to pay attention to what we're thinking about. We need to examine every thought and only choose to think on things which are in alignment with the Word of God. Every thought not in alignment with God's Word, needs to be rejected and denied access to our mind.

Romans 8:5-6 (NLT) "Those who are dominated by the sinful nature think about sinful things, but those who are controlled by the Holy Spirit think about things that please the Spirit. So letting your sinful nature control your mind leads to death. But letting the Spirit control your mind leads to life and peace."

Romans 12:2 (NLT) "Don't copy the behavior and customs of this world, but let God transform you into a new person by changing the way you think. Then you will learn to know God's will for you, which is good and pleasing and perfect."

Even if you have never studied the Bible, you will have an innate knowledge as to whether your thoughts are in alignment with Gods righteousness or not. However, the more time you spend studying the Bible, the more of God's Word you'll get in your heart. When your heart is full of God's Word, you'll be able to instantly examine your thoughts and take them captive according to the Word.

John 8:31-32 (NLT) "Jesus said to the people who believed in him, 'You are truly my disciples if you remain faithful to my teachings. And you will know the truth, and the truth will set you free.'"

It's going to take effort on our part to control our thoughts. However, we can take comfort in knowing that God never tells us to do something that we can't do and the Holy Spirt always dwells within us to help us.

When a thought comes into our mind, which is not in alignment with the Word of God, we need to cast down or reject that thought immediately. We do not have to accept the thought as our own. We need to speak aloud to the thought.

You can say "Satan, in the name of Jesus Christ, I cast your thoughts out of my mind. You have no authority over me. I choose to only think thoughts which are in alignment with the Word of God."

It's important we actually speak these words aloud. Throughout the Apostles (the books of Matthew, Mark, Luke and John) it's written how Jesus took authority over Satan and demons by speaking the Word aloud. It is also written that we have the same authority, through Jesus.

Matt 17:20 (NLT) "... I tell you the truth, if you had faith even as small as a mustard seed, you could say to this mountain, 'Move from here to there' and it would move. Nothing would be impossible.'"

Proverbs 18:21 (NKJV) "Death and life are in the power of the tongue..."

Not only do we want to take our thoughts captive and speak aloud to them, but we also want to replace our thoughts with Godly thoughts.

Philippians 4:8 (NLT) "And now, dear brothers and sisters, one final thing. Fix your thoughts on what is true, and honorable, and right, and pure, and lovely, and admirable. Think about things that are excellent and worthy of praise."

Colossians 3:2 (NLT) "Think about the things of heaven, not the things of earth."

If a Godly thought does not come to mind, think about all God has done for you and start praising Him for all of your blessings, small and large. Praise Him for the food on your table, the roof over your head, the clothes on your back, the clean water you have access to, your good health. Never be too busy with everyday life to not notice all God has done for you.

Chapter 12

Studying the Word

Because our mind is not transformed when we receive salvation, we need to renew our mind. God gives us instructions in the Bible about how we can renew our mind and one of the ways we accomplish this is by studying the Word of God.

When you want to build a relationship with someone, you spend time with that person. It's the same with God. To have a close relationship with Him, to really get to know Him, you need to make Him a priority in your life and spend time with Him by studying His Word.

2 Peter 1:3-9 (NLT) "By his divine power, God has given us everything we need for living a godly life. We have received all of this by coming to know him, the one who called us to himself by means of his marvelous glory and excellence. And because of his glory and excellence, he has given us great and precious promises. These are the promises that enable you to share his divine nature and escape the world's corruption caused by human desires."

Joshua 1:8 (NLT) "Study this Book of Instruction continually. Meditate on it day and night so you will be sure to obey everything written in it. Only then will you prosper and succeed in all you do."

God's thoughts are revealed in the Bible. It shows us what's wrong with our lives, gives us clear instructions about how to change our lives and how we should live our lives.

2 Timothy 3:16 (NLT) "All Scripture is inspired by God and is useful to teach us what is true and to make us realize what is wrong in our lives. It corrects us when we are wrong and teaches us to do what is right."

Because all scripture is inspired by God, the Bible is one of the methods God uses to speak to us. In Mark, Jesus tells his disciples to pay close attention when they hear the Word of God.

Mark 4:24-25 (NLT) Then he added, "Pay close attention to what you hear. The closer you listen, the more understanding you will be given and you will receive even more. To those who listen to my teaching, more understanding will be given. But for those who are not listening, even what little understanding they have will be taken away from them."

The closer attention we pay to what we read in the Bible the more understanding the Holy Spirit will give us about what we're reading. Sometimes when we're reading a passage in the Bible, it might be one we've read several times before, all of a sudden we will receive a new revelation of its meaning. That is the Holy Spirit working in our lives, pointing something out that we need to understand.

The Word is alive, God talks to us through the Bible.

Before starting your Bible study time, pray to God and ask Him to reveal what He wants you to see in each verse.

There is a big difference between reading the Bible and really taking the time to study the Bible. Read for quality, not quantity. Read each verse slowly. Think about each verse and how it applies to you and your life. Is there a new character God wants to develop in you? Is there something He wants to change about you or your life? Is He giving you some type of direction for your life?

Hebrews 4:12 (AMP) "For the Word that God speaks is alive and full of power (making it active, operative, energizing, and effective); it is sharper than any two-edged sword, penetrating to the dividing line of the breath of life (soul) and (the immortal) spirit, and of joints and marrow (of the deepest parts of our nature), exposing and sifting and analyzing and judging thoughts and purposes of the heart."

Psalm 119:98-100 (NLT) "Your commands make me wiser than my enemies, for they are my constant guide. Yes, I have more insight than my teachers, for I am always thinking of your laws. I am even wiser than my elders, for I have kept your commandments."

Studying the Bible will also make us aware when someone is trying to teach or preach "false doctrine," a principle which is not actually in the Bible.

We're also told in Romans 10:17 that we can increase

our faith by studying the Bible.

Romans 10:17 (NLT) "So faith comes from hearing, that is, hearing the Good News about Christ."

There are many different versions of the Bible. I like reading the New Living Translation because the wording used in it is contemporary. I also like the New International Version of the Life Application Study Bible, it has a lot of useful commentary. The third Bible I study is Joyce Meyer's The Everyday Life Bible[15], this is an Amplified Bible containing teaching notes from Joyce Meyer. The amplification in this Bible sometimes gives you a better insight into a scriptures real meaning.

Chapter 13

Hearing the Word

Another biblical principle we can use to renew our mind is hearing the Word of God.

Proverbs 4:20-22 (NLT) "My child, pay attention to what I say. Listen carefully to my words. Don't lose sight of them. Let them penetrate deep into your heart, for they bring life to those who find them, and healing to their whole body."

Pray to God and ask him to direct you to a Spirit filled, Bible teaching church. One in which scripture is the focus of the sermons.

There are also some very good Bible Preachers with programs on television. I enjoy watching: Joyce Meyer's "Enjoying Every Day Life", Dr. Charles Stanley's[16] "In Touch Ministries", Kenneth Copeland's[17] "Kenneth Copeland Ministries", Bishop T.D. Jakes'[18] "The Potter's Touch" and Robert Morris' "The Blessed Life."

Just make sure that whomever you choose to listen to is delivering their sermons based upon Biblical Scripture. Be mindful of what any Preacher teaches and make sure you can find his/her principles in your Bible.

Beware of listening to a preacher or attending a church where it is taught homosexuality is an acceptable lifestyle. Such a preacher or church is not standing on Biblical Truth.

Jude 4 (NLT) "I say this because some ungodly people have wormed their way into your churches, saying that God's marvelous grace allows us to live immoral lives. The condemnation of such people was recorded long ago, for they have denied our only Master and Lord, Jesus Christ."

2 Peter 2:1-2 (NLT) "But there were also false prophets in Israel, just as there will be false teachers among you. They will cleverly teach destructive heresies and even deny the Master who bought them. In this way, they will bring sudden destruction on themselves. Many will follow their evil teaching and shameful immorality. And because of these teachers, the way of truth will be slandered."

1 Timothy 4:1 (NLT) "Now the Holy Spirit tells us clearly that in the last times some will turn away from the true faith; they will follow deceptive spirits and teachings that come from demons."

Whenever goats grazing in a field perceive a threat, they gather together in a tight circle. There is safety for them in the herd. If a goat is separated from the herd, it is vulnerable to attack by predators.

Peter tells us, in 1 Peter, that we need to watch out and stay alert, because Satan roams the earth prowling like a roaring lion, looking for someone to devour. There is safety in numbers and there is safety for believers when they are connected to a church.

You might feel apprehensive about attending church, just like I did. Maybe this apprehension comes from your past encounters with "Christians" waving signs, yelling at you and treating you disrespectfully. If this has happened in the past, I want to apologize to you for their behavior.

When Jesus was asked what was the greatest of the commandments, he stated: to love God with all of your heart, soul and mind. He said the second greatest commandment was to love your neighbor as you love yourself.

Matt 22: 37-40 (NLT) "Jesus replied, 'You must love the LORD your God with all your heart, all your soul, and all your mind.' This is the first and greatest commandment. A second is equally important: 'Love your neighbor as yourself.' The entire law and all the demands of the prophets are based on these two commandments."

"Christian" demonstrators who yell at and harass homosexuals are not acting according to Scripture. They are not acting in love and I really question if they have actually received salvation. Just because someone calls themselves a Christian, does not make them a Christian. Christian should be known for shinning their light on the world, not for acting out in hatred or anger.

If you're apprehensive about attending church because

you think you've been too sinful in the past, remember that upon receiving your salvation, God no longer remembers your sins; and the church pews are full of people with pasts. We are all sinful people, from the Pastors to the Sunday School Teachers.

If you find a church where a Pastor is willing to be honest about his/her struggles, more than likely the congregation will be honest about their struggles.

Ezekiel 28 indicates that Satan was the Praise and Worship Leader in heaven before his fall.

Ezekiel 28:13 (NKJV) "You were in Eden, the garden of God; Every precious stone was our covering: The sardius, topaz, and diamond, beryl, onyx, and jasper, sapphire, turquoise, and emerald with gold. The workmanship of your timbrels and pipes was prepared for you on the day you were created."

A timbrel was an ancient percussion instrument similar to a modern day tambourine. Pipes probably refers to some type of device air was blown through to make a sound. Satan was created with timbrels and pipes built into him.

Satan is very skillful at using music to manipulate our feelings and interject thoughts into our mind. I know if I hear a song from the past, immediately my thoughts are brought back to who I was with or what I was doing the last time I heard that song. Music also has the ability to influence my moods.

It's very important that you're mindful of the type of music you listen to.

I only listen to contemporary Christian music. Christian music has many different formats: soft rock, gospel, rap, soul, bluegrass, southern gospel, hard rock and hymns. So whatever style of music you enjoy listening to you should be able to find a type of Christian music which is enjoyable for you.

I also recommend attending a good Bible Study. Again, make sure that Biblical principles are being taught in the Bible Study.

There are many great teachings available through different ministries throughout the United States.

Chapter 14

The Power of Confessing the Word

Confessing the Word is another biblical principle we can use to renew our mind. Remember God's Word is alive. There is power in confessing the Word of God.

Proverbs 22:17-18 (NLT) "Listen to the words of the wise; apply your heart to my instruction. For it is good to keep these sayings in your heart and always ready on your lips."

In James 3:6, we're told that our tongue (confessions) sets the course for our lives.

We believe what we hear ourselves say more than what we hear anyone else say, so we need to be mindful about what comes out of our mouths. Negative words from our mouths bring curses into our lives and positive words from our mouths bring blessings into our lives. So in essence, what we experience in our lives, either positive or negative, is the result of the words we choose to speak.

Proverbs 13:2 (NLT) "From the fruit of his lips a man enjoys good things…"

Proverbs 18:21 (NLT) "The tongue has the power of life and death …"

Find a promise in God's Word for whatever change you're seeking in yourself or your life, then start confessing the scripture aloud and believe you have received whatever you're confessing.

You might consider confessing, "Greater is He who lives in me than he who is in the world" or "I'm a new person in Christ."

1 John 4:4 (NIV) "You, dear children, are from God and have overcome them (evil spirits), because the one who lives in you (the Holy Spirit) is greater than the one in the world (Satan)."

2 Corinthians 5:17 (NLT) "This means that anyone who belongs to Christ has become a new person. The old life is gone; a new life has begun!"

Always make sure your confession is positive and faith building.

I have taken scriptures and personalized them into my own confession. I used scriptures which referenced changes I wanted to see in my life. I try to confess the following on a daily basis:

"I cast all my cares on you Lord, for you care about me affectionately and watchfully.

I have faith that you can bring all troubles to pass. You give me the peace that surpasses all understanding. You direct my steps and give me strength. You have set me apart and I'm the apple of your eye. You bless me and protect me. You smile upon me and show me your favor. You will not withhold any good thing from me. You have given me a spirit of power, love, a sound mind and self–discipline. You are my strength.

You will liberally supply my every need. I prosper in all things. I'm in good health and my soul prospers.

I freely give forgiveness to others. I'm blessed, happy, fortunate and to be envied because I trust and take refuge in you. I seek my happiness in you. You have great plans for my life. I promptly obey your every command. My ways are pleasing to you and you make my enemies live at peace with me.

I'm committed to you, I lean on you and hope confidently in you. You will guard me and keep me in perfect health with a constant peace. You protect me and surround me with songs of victory. You are my refuge and my fortress. In you I will trust.

I'm slow to anger. I'm kind, humble and disciplined.

My body is your temple and I bring glory to you by tak-ing care of it.

You are my refuge, fortress and high tower. Your ways are perfect. In all my ways, I know, recognize, and acknowledge you. I'm blessed, happy, fortunate, to be envied, because I seek you above all else. I earnestly wait for you, I expect, look and long for you, for your vic-tory, your favor, your love, your peace, your joy and your unbroken companionship. I hear from you, receive in-

struction and accept correction. You grant me wisdom. I renew my mind daily and I'm a new creature in you.

I live by faith, not by sight. You came so that I might have and enjoy life, and have it in abundance.

You are my strength and shield. My heart trust in, relies on and confidently leans on you and I am helped. Therefore, my heart greatly rejoices and with my songs will I praise you."

There are a lot of great books on the market about confessing the Word. One of my favorites is Joyce Meyer's <u>The Secret Power of Speaking God's Word</u>[19].

Chapter 15

The Power of Prayer

We have the awesome privilege of communicating with God, through our prayers, 24/7. Because God hears and answers our prayers, our prayers are important weapons in our battle with Satan.

Praying also brings peace to our lives, because we are turning over our cares to God and placing them on His broad shoulders. We acknowledge that we're not capable of handling our lives and acknowledging that God is the only one capable of handling everything. Nothing is too small or too large for Him. We should also praise God during our prayer time.

Philippians 4:6-7 (NIV) "Do not be anxious about anything, but in everything, by prayer and petition, with thanksgiving, present your request to God. And the peace of God, which transcends all understanding, will guard your hearts and your mind in Christ Jesus."

2 Chronicles 7:14-15 (NLT) "Then if my people who are called by my name will humble themselves and pray and seek my face and turn away from their wicked ways, I will forgive their sins and restore their land. My eyes will be open and my ears attentive to every prayer made in this place."

James 5:16-17 (NIV) "...The prayer of a righteous man is powerful and effective. Elijah was just like us. He prayed earnestly that it would not rain, and it did not rain on the land for three and a half years."

Many times in the New Testament we find Jesus praying to God about many concerns, including direction, provision, intersession, and wisdom, to name just a few. Jesus told his disciples that praying to God could help keep them from temptation.

Matthew 26:41 (NIV) "Watch and pray so that you will not fall into temptation. The spirit is willing, but the body is weak."

We can follow these examples and pray to God, bring our concerns to Him, asking Him for direction, provision, forgiveness, wisdom, or help with keeping us from temptations.

In John 15:16, Jesus tells us that because we have accepted him as our Lord and Savior, when we pray to God we should make are request in Jesus' name. We can't come to God in prayer under or own authority; we are only allowed that access under Jesus' authority. So when I pray, I end my prayers with "I say this in Jesus precious name, Amen." Amen means 'so be it.'

Your prayers do not have to be formal. God wants to be included in your everyday life, talk (pray) to Him throughout your day. Remember He loves you and wants you to lean on Him.

Prayers can also be used for breaking strongholds. A friend of mine, aware of my struggles, gave me a book written by Liberty Savard, <u>Shattering Your Strongholds</u>[20]. While reading the book I realized I had built strongholds around my homosexual lifestyle and I had the authority, under Jesus Christ, to remove those strongholds through prayer. I found the following prayer, which I try to confess on a daily basis, in this book:

"In the name of Jesus Christ, I bind my body, soul and spirit to the will and purposes of God. I bind myself to an awareness of the power of the blood of Jesus working in my life every day. I bind my mind to the mind of Christ so I can have the thoughts, purposes and feelings of His mind and heart in me. I bind my feet to the paths you have ordained for me to walk, God, that my steps will be strong and steady. I bind myself to the work of the cross with all of its mercy, truth, love, power, forgiveness and dying to self. I know that this is where the power to become a new creature in Christ lies.

Lord, I repent of having wrong attitudes and thoughts: I renounce them now and ask for your forgiveness. I loose every old, wrong, pattern of thinking, attitude, idea, desire, belief, habit and behavior that may still be working in me. I tear down, crush, smash, and destroy every stronghold I have erected to protect them. I bind myself to the attitudes of Jesus Christ.

Father, I loose the power and the effects of any harsh or hard words (word curses) spoken about me, to me, or by me. I loose any stronghold thinking still connected to them. I loose all generational bondage thinking from myself. Thank you, Jesus, that you have promised that whatever I bind and loose on earth, that is in accordance with the will of the Father, will be bound and loosed in heaven. Amen"

Paul tells us in Ephesians 6 that we need to put on the full armor of God to be successful in our battle with Satan. Basically, Paul was trying to describe God's biblical principles for battling Satan, in terms of the armor a Roman solider would use while fighting an enemy.

Ephesians 6:10-13 (NLT) "A final word: Be strong in the Lord and in his mighty power. Put on all of God's armor so that you will be able to stand firm against all strategies of the devil. For we are not fighting against flesh-and-blood enemies, but against evil rulers and authorities of the unseen world, against mighty powers in this dark world, and against evil spirits in the heavenly places. Therefore, put on every piece of God's armor so you will be able to resist the enemy in the time of evil. Then after the battle you will still be standing firm."

I found the following prayer in Dr. Charles Stanley book <u>Temptation</u>[21]. This is a great prayer and confession, for putting on the armor of God, in our daily battle with Satan. I can't stress enough how important it is for you to pray this prayer or one similar to it on a daily basis. I recommend that you make a copy of it and start each morning with it.

"Good morning, Lord. Thank You for assuring me victory today if I will but follow Your battle plan. So by faith I claim victory over _____ (I recommend you list

any temptation you're dealing with).

To prepare myself for the battle ahead, by faith I put on the belt of truth. The truth about You, Lord-that You are a sovereign God who knows everything about me, both my strengths and my weaknesses. Lord, You know my breaking point and have promised not to allow me to be tempted beyond what I may bear. The truth about me, Lord, is that I am a new creature in Christ and have been set free from the power of sin. I am indwelt with the Holy Spirit who will guide me and warn me when danger is near. I am Your child, and nothing can separate me from Your love. The truth is that You have a purpose for me this day-someone to encourage, someone to share with, someone to love.

Next Lord, I want to, by faith, put on the breastplate of righteousness. Through this I guard my heart and my emotions. I will not allow my heart to attach itself to anything that is impure. I will not allow my emotions to rule in my decisions. I will set them on what is right and good and just. I will live by what is true, not by what I feel.

Lord, this morning I put on the sandals of the gospel of peace. I am available to You, Lord. Send me where You will. Guide me to those who need encouragement or physical help of some kind. Use me to solve conflicts wherever they may arise. Make me a calming presence in every circumstance in which You place me. I will not be hurried or rushed, for my schedule is in Your hands. I will not leave a trail of tension and apprehension. I will leave tracks of peace and stability everywhere I go.

I now take up the shield of faith, Lord. My faith is in You and You alone. Apart from You, I can do nothing. With You, I can do all things. No temptation that comes my way can penetrate Your protecting hand. I will not be afraid, for You are going with me throughout this day. When I am tempted I will claim victory out loud ahead of time, for You have promised victory to those who walk in obedience to Your Word. So by faith I claim victory even now because I know there are fiery darts headed my way even as I pray. Lord, You already know what they are and have already provided the way of escape.

Lord, by faith I am putting on the helmet of salvation. You know how Satan bombards my mind day and night with evil thoughts, doubt and fear. I put on this helmet that will protect my mind. I may feel the impact of his attacks, but nothing can penetrate this helmet. I choose to stop every impure and negative thought at the door of my mind. And with the helmet of salvation those thoughts will get no further. I elect to take every thought captive; I will dwell on nothing but what is good and right and pleasing to You.

Last, I take up the sword of the Spirit, which is Your Word. Thank You for the precious gift of Your Word. It is strong and powerful and able to defeat even the strongest of Satan's onslaughts. Your Word says that I am not under obligation to the flesh to obey its lusts. Your Word says that I am free from the power of sin. Your Word says that He that is in me is greater that he who is in the world. So by faith I take up the strong and powerful sword of the Spirit, which is able to defend me in time of attack, comfort me in time of sorrow, teach me in time of meditation, and prevail against the power of the enemy on behalf of others who need the truth to set them free.

So, Lord, I go now rejoicing that You have chosen me to represent You to this lost and dying world. May others see Jesus in me, and may Satan and his hosts shudder as Your power is made manifest in me. In Jesus' name I pray-AMEN"

Chapter 16

Guarding Our Sight

Another method Satan uses to tempt us involves our sight. Part of Eve's temptation, in the Garden of Eden, was looking at and finding the forbidden fruit pleasing to her eyes.

Genesis 3:6 (NIV) "When the woman (Eve) saw that the (forbidden) fruit of the tree was good food and pleasing to the eye, and also desirable for gaining wisdom, she took some and ate it."

Satan is skillful at presenting opportunities for us to see things which results in lustful thoughts. Be on guard at what you look at.

Mark 9:47 (NLT) "And if your eye causes you to sin, gouge it out. It's better to enter the Kingdom of God with only one eye than to have two eyes and be thrown into hell,"

1 John 2:16 (NLT) "For the world (Satan) offers only a craving for physical pleasure, a craving for everything we see, and pride in our achievements and possessions. These are not from the Father, but are from this world."

Luke 11:34-35 (AMP) "The eye is the lamp of your

body. When your eye is clear [spiritually perceptive, focused on God], your whole body also is full of light [benefiting from God's precepts]. But when it is bad [spiritually blind], your body also is full of darkness [devoid of God's word]. Be careful, therefore, that the light that is in you is not darkness."

We should restrain from reading homosexual novels or erotica, cruising homosexual dating sites on the web or watching pornography. We should also be mindful of the movies and television shows we choose to watch. We do not have to watch movies or television shows which contain sexual scenes or homosexual themes.

What should we do when we're tempted to look at something that might cause a lustful response in us? Look away! Don't take that second glance. Be mindful and guard your eyes.

Proverbs 4:25 (NLT) "Look straight ahead, and fix your eyes on what lies before you."

Chapter 17

Fasting

Fasting, is deliberately abstaining from something pleasurable for a specific period of time to honor God. In essence we're saying God I need you more than anything else in my life. When we honor God, He honors us. Fasting draws us into a deeper relationship with God and can also be used to seek God's will in any given situation.

Among some of the things we can fast from are food (specific types of food, a meal, or going without eating for one or several days), watching television, using our smart phones, or using the internet, basically any activity we find pleasurable.

In Matthew 6:16, Jesus does not tell us if you fast, he tells us "when you fast." Fasting is an expected activity if you're a believer in Jesus Christ.

Our body is God's temple. We're no longer our own, Jesus bought us with his blood. Since our body is God's temple, we need to glorify God with our bodies by keeping them holy and free from evil.

Romans 6:13 (NLT) "Do not let any part of your body become an instrument of evil to serve sin. Instead, give yourselves completely to God, for you were dead, but now you have new life. So use your whole body as an instrument to do what is right for the glory of God."

1 Corinthians 3:16 (NLT) "God will destroy anyone who destroys this temple. For God's temple is holy, and you are that temple."

Remember, man is a spirit, he has a soul (consisting of mind, will and emotions) and he lives in a body. Man's spirit has control over his soul and his soul has control over his body.

When we received salvation, our spirit was born again. However, because our body was not born again at salvation, we need to bring it under the submission of our reborn spirit. We also need to discipline our bodies and present them to God as a holy sacrifice.

Romans 12:1 (NIV) "Therefore, I urge you, brothers, in view of God's mercy, to offer your bodies as living sacrifices, holy and pleasing to God-this is your spiritual act of worship..."

When we lived our lives as homosexuals, we were living by our fleshly lustful desires. The Amplified Bible describes flesh as our godless human nature.

1 Corinthians 6:18-20 (NLT) "Run from sexual sin! No other sin affects the body as this one does. For sexual immorality is a sin against your own body. Don't you realize that your body is the temple of the Holy Spirit, who lives in you and was given to you by God? You do

not belong to yourself, for God bought you with a high price. So you must honor God with your body."

Fasting from food can be used to draw us closer to God by teaching us how to gain control of our physical desires and bring them under the submission of our reborn spirit. This results in bringing honor to God.

Successfully completing a fast gives us confidence that we can control our own fleshly desires.

Chapter 18

What to Do When We Experience
A Same-Sex Attraction (SSA)

First, we need to realize that upon receiving salvation we came under the authority of Jesus Christ. What this means is that although we might still experience a SSA, since we are now under the authority of Jesus Christ, we no longer have to give into the SSA because we have been set free from sin's power over us.

Paul tells us that when Jesus was crucified he died to sin, he permanently removed sin's authority in our lives.

Romans 6:10-11 (NIV) "The death he died, he died to sin once and for all; but the life he lives, he lives to God. In the same way, count yourselves dead to sin but alive to God in Christ Jesus."

Romans 6:14 (NIV) "For sin shall not be your master, because you are not under the law, but under grace."

However, being set free from sin's authority over us does not mean that we've been set free from temptations. Because of the sinful nature of earth, Satan will never stop trying to tempt us.

What we also need to realize, is that being tempted is

not the same as sinning. After being baptized, Jesus was led into the desert for 40 days were he was tempted by Satan. We know Jesus never sinned.

2 Corinthians 5:21 (NLT) "For God made Christ, who never sinned, to be the offering for our sin, so that we could be made right with God through Christ."

When experiencing a SSA, we cross over the line into sin when we choose to engage our mind in lustful thoughts about the object of our attraction. Remember, Satan attacks us in our thoughts. What we choose to think about grows. Once we have engaged our mind in lustful sexual thoughts, we have sinned. Everywhere in the Bible where we read a reference to lust, that lust results in sin.

In Matthew, Jesus tells us that if a man even looks at a woman with lust, he has already committed adultery with that woman. The sin is first committed with thoughts in the mind.

Matthew 5:28 (NLT) "But I say, anyone who even looks at a woman with lust has already committed adultery with her in his heart."

So the most important tool we can use when dealing with a SSA, is to guard our thoughts and imaginations. This is the area we need to be very disciplined in. We need to control our mind and not allow ourselves to engage in lustful thoughts. Every time we catch ourselves thinking about the SSA, we need to stop! We need to closely monitor our thoughts to keep them in check.

We need to also replace our SSA thoughts with thoughts in alignment with the Word of God.

Colossians 3:2 (NLT) "Think about the things of heaven, not the things of earth."

Philippians 4:8 (NLT) "And now, dear brothers and sisters, one final thing. Fix your thoughts on what is true, and honorable, and right, and pure, and lovely, and admirable. Think about things that are excellent and worthy of praise."

We need to make sure we never confess our SSA to the person we're attracted to. Our confession cracks the door for Satan to gain a foothold.

What we can confess aloud, when we experience a SSA, is that we are a new creature in Christ and we choose to live our lives in alignment with the Word of God.

Keep the SSA in the proper perspective; it's just another attempt by Satan to lead us into sin. We don't have to take ownership of the SSA.

If we experience a SSA, we should not come under condemnation from Satan. Satan will be right there interjecting thoughts into our mind: like, 'we haven't been successful at leaving the lifestyle,' 'we're not really saved' and 'we have to give in to our feelings.' Remember Satan is a liar!

All too often in the past we let our feelings control us.

When experiencing a SSA, the feelings we experience might be familiar to the person we used to be, but we are no longer that person. We need to remember that our feelings are no more than an emotional response to a stimulus. Our feelings are not to be trusted. We can feel something one moment and then feel something totally different the next moment.

Just because we might feel something strongly, does not mean that we have to let our feelings control the direction of our lives. We need to get beyond our feelings and allow our thoughts, in alignment with the Word of God, control the direction of our lives. We need to remember, what we might feel in any given moment has nothing to do with the absolute truth of the Word.

I heard Joyce Meyer recently say "Let's stop worshiping our feelings and start worshiping our God."

So when you experience a SSA, relax, calm down and take a breath. Satan is not in control, Jesus is. You're not alone, the Holy Spirit is right there beside you and he's not going anywhere.

Know that you're not the only one who has experienced a SSA after coming out of a homosexual lifestyle. Experiencing SSA is not unusual. The more successful you are at controlling your thought life, the quicker the SSA will subside. The longer you have been out of the homosexual lifestyle, the less frequently you will experience a SSA.

Remember you are a child of the most high God.

Joshua 1:9 (NLT) "This is my command – be strong and courageous! Do not be afraid or discouraged. For the Lord your God is with you wherever you go."

Chapter 19

Making New Friends

When you lived a homosexual lifestyle, you immersed yourself in the homosexual environment. You attended homosexual events, had homosexual friends and probably read material and watched movies with homosexual themes.

If you're serious about wanting to leave the homosexual lifestyle, you really need to remove yourself from the homosexual environment. If you were an alcoholic and you wanted to stay sober, it wouldn't make any sense for you to hang out with your old drinking buddies at the bar.

The same is true if you're coming out of a homosexual lifestyle. Remember you have previously been under Satan's control and have strongholds in your mind in this area of your life.

Ephesians 2:2, tells us that Satan's spirit is the spirit at work in the hearts of those who refuse to obey God. That means Satan's spirit is at work in the hearts of your homosexual friends. Because your old friend's minds have not been renewed with the Holy Spirit, their thinking is ungodly and Satan can use them to try and gain authority over your life again.

Satan even used Peter, one of Jesus disciples, in an attempt to destroy God's plan for salvation.

Mark 8:31-33 (NLT) "Then Jesus began to tell them that the Son of Man must suffer many terrible things and be rejected by the elders, the leading priests, and the teachers of religious law. He would be killed, but three days later he would raise from the dead. As he talked about this openly with his disciples, Peter took him aside and began to reprimand him for saying such things. Jesus turned around and looked at his disciples, then reprimanded Peter. 'Get away from me, Satan!' He said. 'You see things merely from a human point of view, not from God's.'"

Psalm 1:1 (Amp) "Blessed (Happy, fortunate, prosperous, and enviable) is the man who walks and lives not in the counsel of the ungodly (following their advice, their plans and purposes), nor stands (submissive and inactive) in the path where sinners walk, nor sits down (to relax and rest) where the scornful (and the mockers) gather."

Don't attend homosexual events or go to homosexual bars.

Make new Christian friends. Pray and ask God to bring some new friends, who will not tempt you, into your life.

Beware of becoming involved in a heterosexual relationship prior to gaining freedom from your homosexual lifestyle. If you become involved in a relationship too soon, your attention might be diverted from doing the work that's necessary to gain freedom from your old life-style, to focusing on your new relationship.

Also remember, if you've received salvation, you never have to feel lonely because you're never alone. The Holy Spirit resides within you.

Chapter 20

What if You Have a Homosexual Relative or Friend

Again I want to point out, when Jesus was asked what was the greatest of the commandments, he stated, "to love God with all of your heart, soul and mind." He said the second greatest commandment was to "love your neighbor as you love yourself."

Matt 22: 37-40 (NLT) "Jesus replied, 'You must love the LORD your God with all your heart, all your soul, and all your mind.' This is the first and greatest commandment. A second is equally important: 'Love your neighbor as yourself.' The entire law and all the demands of the prophets are based on these two commandments.'"

Just because God views homosexuality as evil, does not mean that He views homosexuals as evil. Homosexuals are lost children of God. Christians are called to a life of love, not hatred. As Christians we need to separate the sinner from the sin.

So if you're reading this book because you have a family member or friend living a homosexual lifestyle, never stop praying for that individual. There is always hope. Remember I didn't become a Christian until I was forty-nine years old. When praying for the individual ask for wisdom from God about how to communicate with them about their homosexuality.

Don't be afraid to glorify God to the individual when you spend time with him/her. Talk openly about God, what He's doing in your life and how you have been changed by your relationship with Him.

You can explain to him/her that you know how difficult it is to deal with temptations. Be honest with them about a temptation that you might be dealing with in your life. Explain that we all have struggles with temptations. When we face those struggles, we must decide if we are going to honor God by our actions or are we going to give into the temptation for a moment of temporary pleasure.

If you're a parent of a homosexual, don't take it personally that your son or daughter has disclosed their homosexuality. It is not your fault that your child is choosing to live a homosexual lifestyle.

Also, if you're a parent of a homosexual, you might want to find a support group where you can share your feeling and struggles.

Tell your homosexual relative or friend that it is possible to leave the lifestyle. You can share my story with them and ask them if they would be interested in reading my book or visiting my website www.returnhome.today. There are other books written by former homosexuals. There are also other websites with testimonies from former homosexuals.

I don't recommend supporting the lifestyle by attending homosexual "weddings". If you invite a homosexual couple to your home I don't recommend allowing them to sleep in the same bedroom if they spend the night in your home. God views homosexuality as a sin, you should not encourage or support sinful activities. As Christians we need to take a stand on the absolute truth of God's Word in love.

What if you're afraid to share the truth of the gospel with your loved ones?

Let me bring something to your attention through a fictional story. Suppose you don't tell your loved one the truth and they die. Upon arriving in hell, they are told they are sentenced there for eternity, however, before they start their sentence they are allowed one phone call. They decide to make that one phone call to you because they know you love them and you're a Christian. When you answer their phone call the first thing they ask you is "why didn't you tell me that living my life as a homosexual would result in me spending eternity in hell?"

What are you going to say to them?

If you're a Christian, the Bible has to be the absolute truth in your life. Share the truth of the Word with your loved one in love and with respect and kindness.

Remember you might be the only person standing between them spending an eternity in heaven or spending an eternity in hell.

A Personal Note from the Author

This journey takes time to complete. Be patient with yourself and never forget God is walking right beside you. Don't be afraid to lean on Him and draw upon His strength.

You didn't become engaged in the bondage of homosexually in one day and it's going to take time to successfully leave your lifestyle.

Isaiah 40:31 (NLT) "But those who trust in the Lord will find new strength. They will soar high on wings like eagles. They will run and not grow weary. They will walk and not faint."

Colossians 3:10 (NLT) "Put on your new nature, and be renewed as you learn to know your Creator and become like him."

I left the homosexual lifestyle over eight years ago. If I can do it, so can you. It's possible!

Philippians 4:13 (NKJV) I can do all things through Christ who strengthens me.

If you would like to contact me I can be reached at my ministry: www.returnhome.today.

Notes

Page 5

[1] King James Bible. In 1604, King James I of England authorized a new translation of the Bible into English. (Story Behind King James Bible, Ken Curtis, Ph.D.) http://www.christianity.com/timeline/1601-1700/story-behind-king-james-bible-11630052.html

Page 9

[2] Harvey Milk. Harvey Bernard Milk (May 22, 1930 – November 27, 1978) was an American politician who became the first openly gay person to be elected to public office in California, when he won a seat on the San Francisco Board of Supervisors. Wikipedia https://en.wikipedia.org/wiki/Harvey_Milk

[3] Dan White (September 2, 1946 – October 21, 1985) was a San Francisco supervisor who assassinated San Francisco Mayor George Moscone and Supervisor Harvey Milk, on Monday, November 27, 1978, at City Hall. Wikipedia https://en.wikipedia.org/wiki/Dan_White

Page 12

[4] National Reno Gay Rodeo. The first gay rodeo was held as a charity fundraising event at the Washoe County Fairgrounds in Reno, Nevada on October 2, 1976. Wikia http://lgbt.wikia.com/wiki/National_Reno_Gay_Rodeo

[5] Phil Ragsdale founded the first Reno Gay Rodeo, later known as the National Reno Gay Rodeo. Mr. Ragsdale died of AIDS on June 1, 1992, *Reno Gazette-Journal* June 4, 1992.

Page 13

[6] Joan Rivers (June 8, 1933 – September 4, 2014), was an American actress, comedian, writer, producer, and television host noted for her often controversial comedic persona—where she was alternately self-deprecating or sharply acerbic, especially toward celebrities and politicians. Wikipedia
https://en.wikipedia.org/wiki/Joan_Rivers

Page 14

[7] International Gay Rodeo Association. The International Gay Rodeo Association (IGRA), founded in 1985,[1] is the sanctioning body for gay rodeos held throughout the United States and Canada. Wikipedia
https://en.wikipedia.org/wiki/International_Gay_Rodeo_Association

Page 15

[8] The Golden State Gay Rodeo Association was formed in 1984 by Al Bell and Pat McGrath. The first gay rodeo in the state was begun in March 1985, and was held at the Los Angeles Equestrian Center in Burbank. LGBT project wiki

http://lgbt.wikia.com/wiki/Golden_State_Gay_Rodeo_Association

[9] The IGRA Hall of Fame honors individuals who have provided for the development and growth of gay rodeo, or who have accrued an outstanding record or achieved a prominent position in the sport.
https://www.igra.com/index.htm

Page 17

[10] Joyce Meyer (born Pauline Joyce Hutchison; June 4, 1943) is a Charismatic Christian, author, and speaker. Television ministry, Enjoying Everyday life. Wikipedia
https://en.wikipedia.org/wiki/Joyce_Meyer

Page 18

[11] The Left Behind series is a series of 16 novels (13 of which are best-sellers) by Tim LaHaye and Jerry B. Jenkins. Wikia
http://leftbehind.wikia.com/wiki/Left_Behind_(series)

[12] The New Living Translation Bible. The goal of any Bible translation is to convey the meaning of the ancient Hebrew and Greek texts as accurately as possible to the modern reader.
https://www.biblegateway.com/versions/New-Living-Translation-NLT-Bible/

Page 25

[13] Pastor Robert Morris. Robert Morris pastor evangelis-

tic church in Southlake, Texas, Gateway church. Robert Morris is featured on the weekly television program, The Blessed Life.
https://en.wikipedia.org/wiki/Gateway_Church_(Texas)

Page 32

[14] New International Version of the Life Application Study Bible, Life Application® Study Bible, New International Version®, Copyright © 1988, 1989, 1990, 1991 by Tyndale House Publishers, Inc. Wheaton IL 60189

Page 94

[15] The Every Day Life Bible Additional Text © 2006 Joyce Meyer, Amplified Bible® copyright © 1954, 1958, 1962, 1964, 1965, 1987 by The Lockman Foundation® All rights reserved. Warner Faith Hachette Book Group USA 1271 Avenue of the Americas, New York, NY 10020

Page 95

[16] Dr. Charles Stanley, Charles F. Stanley is the founder of In Touch Ministries and a *New York Times* best-selling author. http://intouch.org/about-us/meet-dr-charles-stanley

[17] Kenneth Copeland, Kenneth Max Copeland (born December 6, 1936) an American author, musician, public speaker, and televangelist. Kenneth Copeland Ministries (KCM).
Https://en.wikipedia.org/wiki/Kenneth_Copeland

[18] Bishop T.D. Jakes Thomas Dexter "T. D." Jakes, Sr. (born June 9, 1957) is an American pastor, author and filmmaker. Bishop of The Potter's House. His evangelistic sermons are broadcast on *The Potter's Touch.*
https://en.wikipedia.org/wiki/T._D._Jakes

Page 104

[19] Meyer, Joyce. 2004. The Secret Power Of Speaking God's Word, Faithworks, New York, NY 10169

Page 107

[20] Savard, Liberty. 1993. Shattering Your Strongholds, Bridge-Logos, P.O. Box 141630, Gainesville, FL 32614

Page 108

[21] Stanley, Charles F. 1988. Temptation, Oliver-Nelson Books, a division of Thomas Nelson, Inc., Publishers, USA.

Made in the USA
Lexington, KY
25 September 2019